CHICKEN WITH PLUMS

BY THE SAME AUTHOR

Persepolis: The Story of a Childhood

Persepolis 2: The Story of a Return

Embroideries

CHICKEN WITH PLUMS

MARJANE SATRAPI

Jonathan Cape
London

Published by Jonathan Cape 2006

4 6 8 10 9 7 5 3

Originally published in France as *PouletAux Prunes* by L' Association, Paris in 2004

Copyright © 2004 by L' Association, 16 rue de la Pierre Levée, 75011 Paris
Translation copyright © 2006 by Anjali Singh

Marjane Satrapi has asserted her right under the Copyright, Designs
and Patents Act, 1988 to be identified as the author of this work

First published in Great Britain in 2006 by
Jonathan Cape
Random House, 20 Vauxhall Bridge Road,
London SW1V 2SA

Addresses for companies within The Random House Group Limited can be found at:
www.randomhouse.co.uk/offices.htm

The Random House Group Limited Reg. No. 954009

A CIP catalogue record for this book
is available from the British Library

ISBN 9780224080453

The Random House Group Limited supports The Forest Stewardship Council
(FSC), the leading international forest certification organisation. All our titles
that are printed on Greenpeace approved FSC certified paper carry the
FSC logo. Our paper procurement policy can be found at:
www.rbooks.co.uk/environment

Printed and bound in Great Britain by
the MPG Books Group, Bodmin, Cornwall

CHICKEN WITH PLUMS

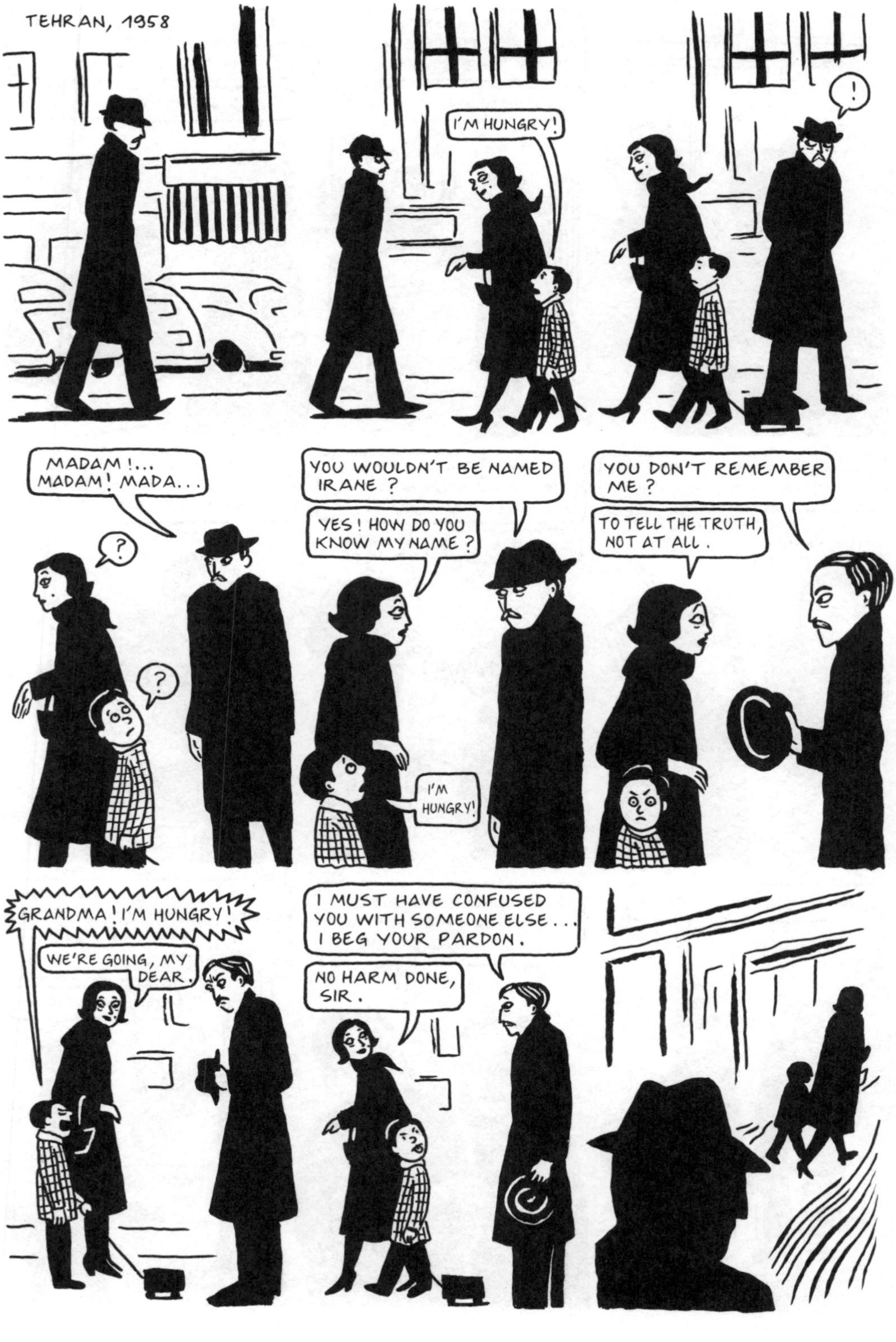
TEHRAN, 1958
I'M HUNGRY!
!
MADAM!... MADAM! MADA...
?
?
YOU WOULDN'T BE NAMED IRANE ?
YES! HOW DO YOU KNOW MY NAME?
I'M HUNGRY!
YOU DON'T REMEMBER ME ?
TO TELL THE TRUTH, NOT AT ALL.
GRANDMA! I'M HUNGRY!
WE'RE GOING, MY DEAR.
I MUST HAVE CONFUSED YOU WITH SOMEONE ELSE... I BEG YOUR PARDON.
NO HARM DONE, SIR.

NASSER ALI KHAN*!!! WHAT AN HONOR TO WELCOME YOU TO MY HUMBLE SHOP!!

MIRZA! I'M LOOKING FOR A TAR.

A TAR?? BUT YOU OWN PROBABLY THE BEST ONE IN THE COUNTRY!

SOMEONE BROKE IT.

IN THE NAME OF GOD! WHO DARED TO BREAK THE TAR OF NASSER ALI KHAN?

CAN I TRY THIS ONE?

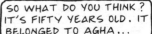

SO WHAT DO YOU THINK? IT'S FIFTY YEARS OLD. IT BELONGED TO AGHA...

TOO LOW...

THE STORE IS DAMP! THAT'S WHY! LISTEN TO THIS ZARB.** IT SOUNDS LIKE AN INDIAN DRUM.

HUMIDITY, I TELL YOU!!

HOW LONG HAVE WE KNOWN EACH OTHER? YOU CAN TRUST ME!

STORE IT IN A VERY DRY PLACE. YOU'LL SEE! AFTER A WEEK, ITS TONE WILL BE PERFECT.

GOOD-BYE MIRZA.

*KHAN MEANS "LORD-SIR."

**IRANIAN PERCUSSION INSTRUMENT.

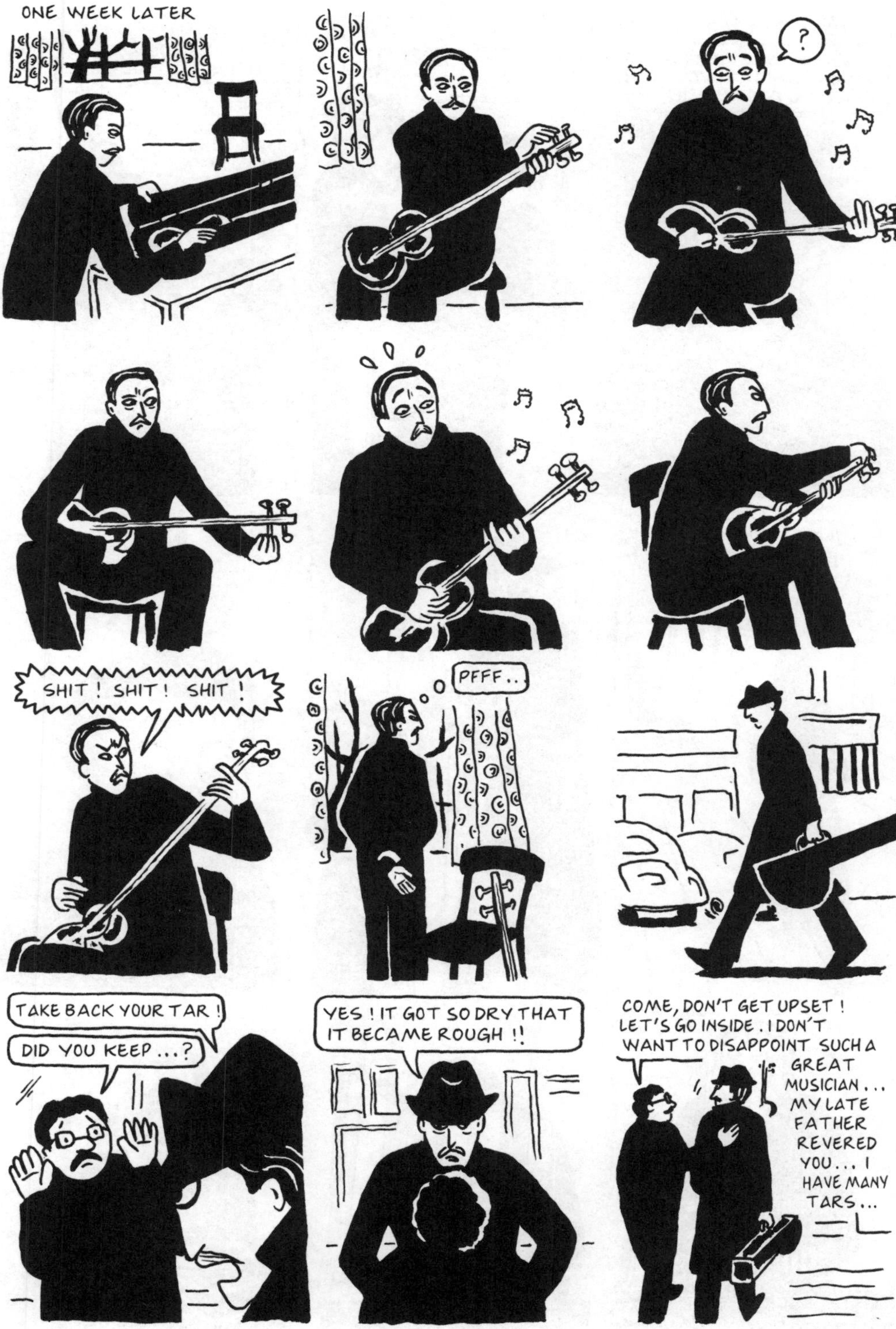
ONE WEEK LATER
?
SHIT! SHIT! SHIT!
PFFF..
TAKE BACK YOUR TAR!
DID YOU KEEP...?
YES! IT GOT SO DRY THAT IT BECAME ROUGH!!
COME, DON'T GET UPSET! LET'S GO INSIDE. I DON'T WANT TO DISAPPOINT SUCH A GREAT MUSICIAN... MY LATE FATHER REVERED YOU... I HAVE MANY TARS...

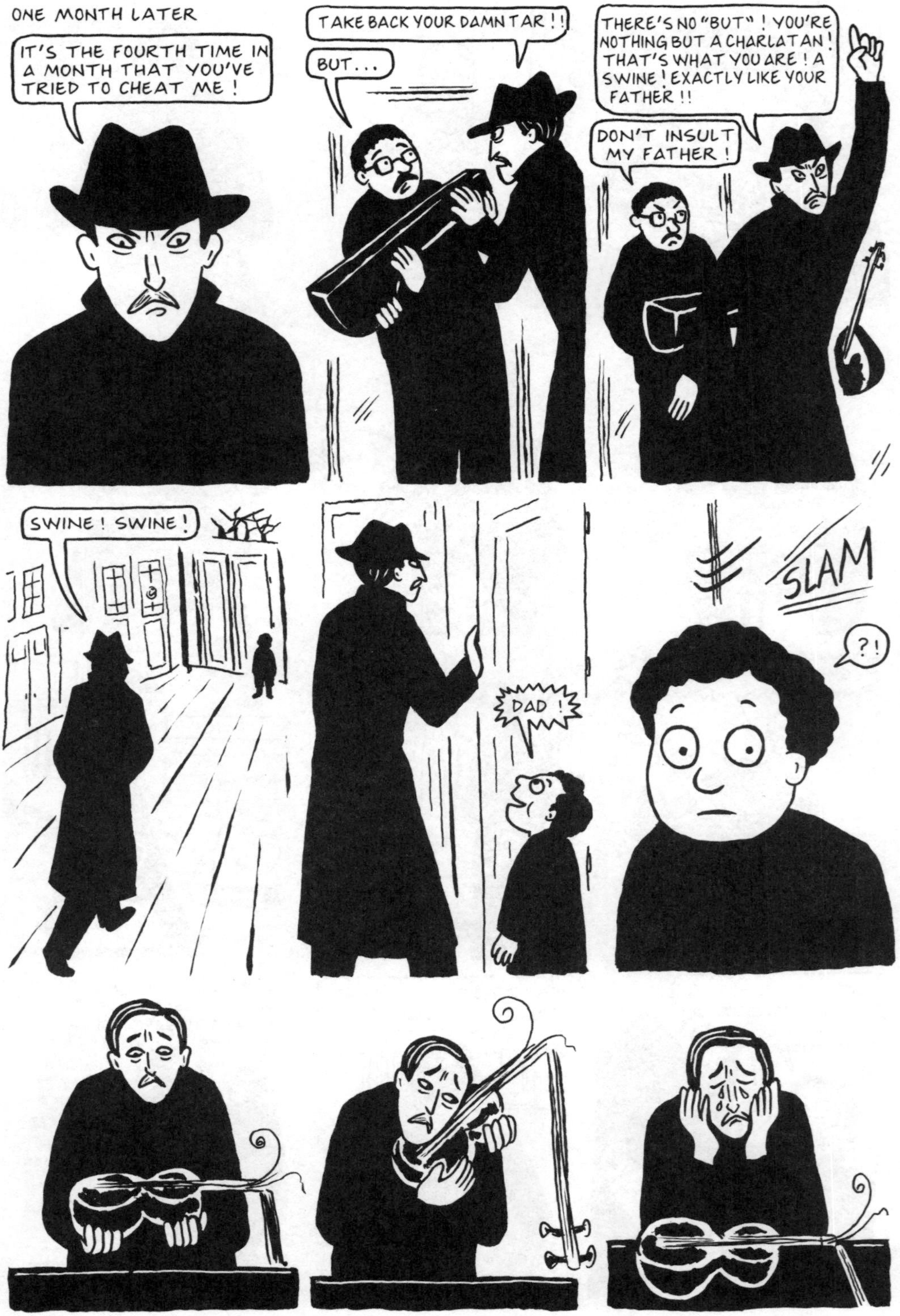
ONE MONTH LATER
IT'S THE FOURTH TIME IN A MONTH THAT YOU'VE TRIED TO CHEAT ME !
TAKE BACK YOUR DAMN TAR !!
BUT...
THERE'S NO "BUT" ! YOU'RE NOTHING BUT A CHARLATAN ! THAT'S WHAT YOU ARE ! A SWINE ! EXACTLY LIKE YOUR FATHER !!
DON'T INSULT MY FATHER !
SWINE ! SWINE !
DAD !
SLAM
?!

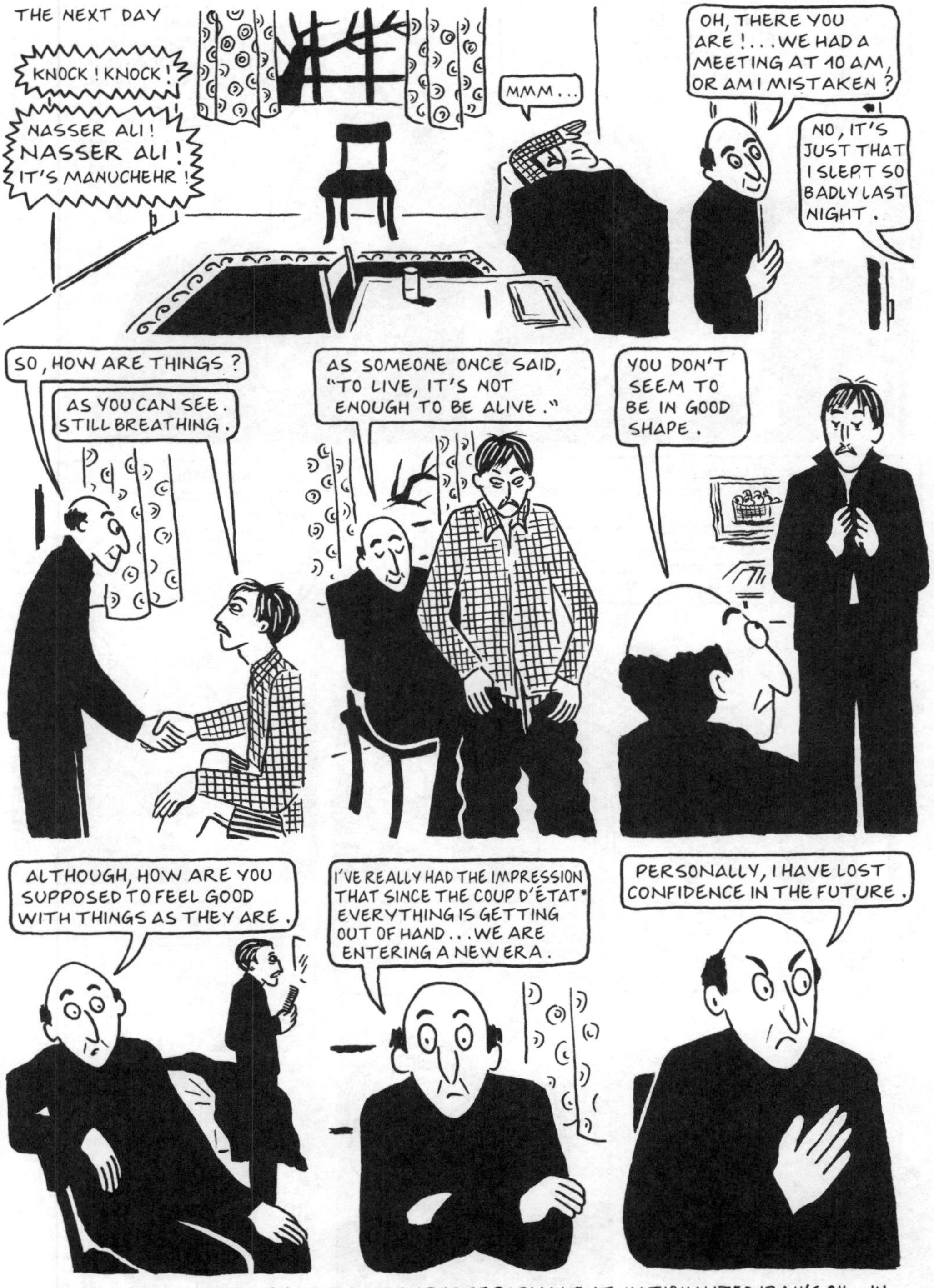
THE NEXT DAY
KNOCK! KNOCK!
NASSER ALI! NASSER ALI! IT'S MANUCHEHR!
MMM...
OH, THERE YOU ARE!... WE HAD A MEETING AT 10 AM, OR AM I MISTAKEN?
NO, IT'S JUST THAT I SLEPT SO BADLY LAST NIGHT.
SO, HOW ARE THINGS?
AS YOU CAN SEE. STILL BREATHING.
AS SOMEONE ONCE SAID, "TO LIVE, IT'S NOT ENOUGH TO BE ALIVE."
YOU DON'T SEEM TO BE IN GOOD SHAPE.
ALTHOUGH, HOW ARE YOU SUPPOSED TO FEEL GOOD WITH THINGS AS THEY ARE.
I'VE REALLY HAD THE IMPRESSION THAT SINCE THE COUP D'ÉTAT* EVERYTHING IS GETTING OUT OF HAND... WE ARE ENTERING A NEW ERA.
PERSONALLY, I HAVE LOST CONFIDENCE IN THE FUTURE.

*IN MARCH 1951, MOSSADEGH, THEN A MEMBER OF PARLIAMENT, NATIONALIZED IRAN'S OIL. IN APRIL OF THE SAME YEAR, HE WAS NAMED PRIME MINISTER. IN AUGUST 1953, MOSSADEGH WAS OUSTED IN A COUP D'ÉTAT INSTIGATED BY THE CIA WITH THE HELP OF THE BRITISH.

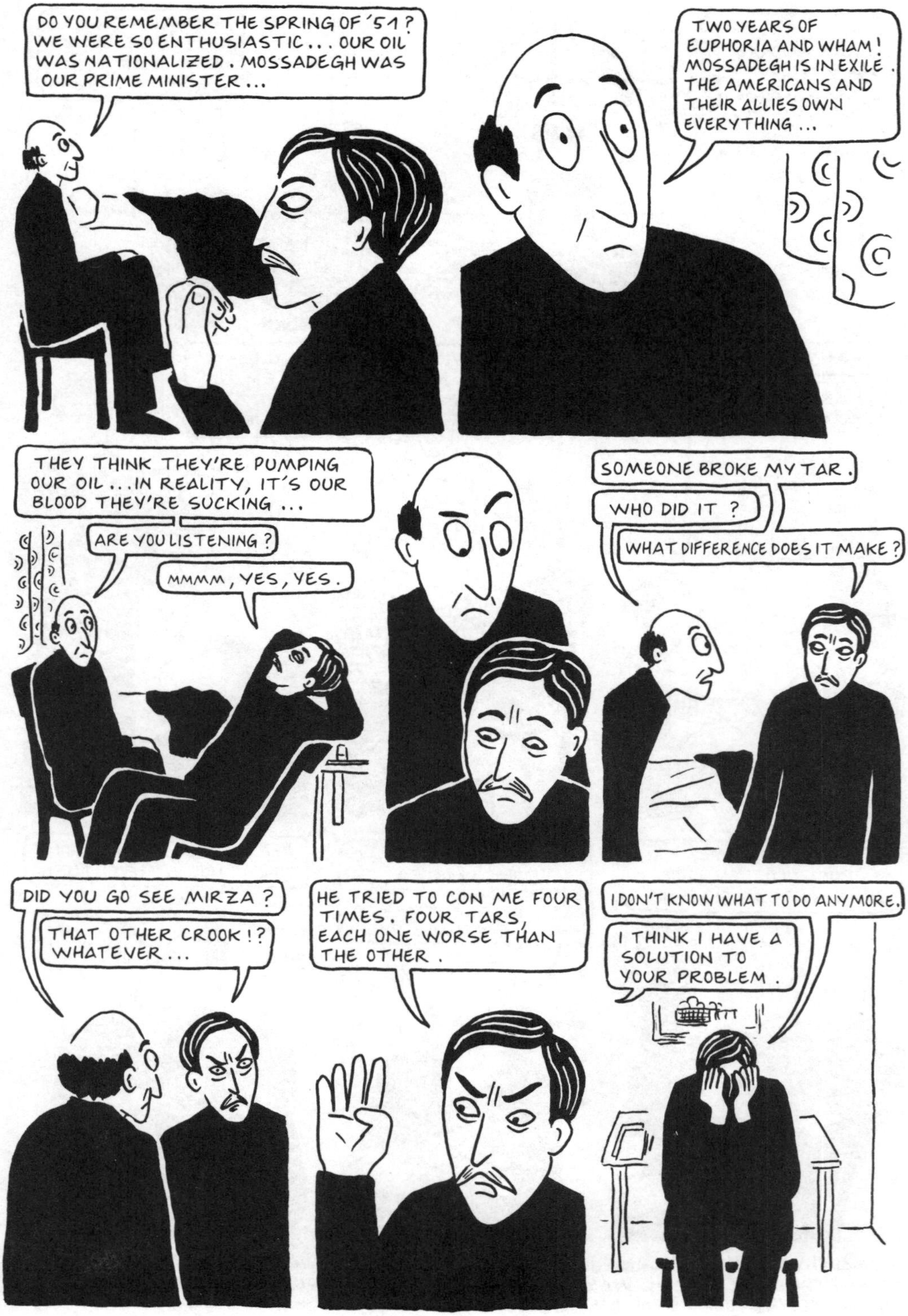
DO YOU REMEMBER THE SPRING OF '51? WE WERE SO ENTHUSIASTIC... OUR OIL WAS NATIONALIZED. MOSSADEGH WAS OUR PRIME MINISTER...
TWO YEARS OF EUPHORIA AND WHAM! MOSSADEGH IS IN EXILE. THE AMERICANS AND THEIR ALLIES OWN EVERYTHING...
THEY THINK THEY'RE PUMPING OUR OIL... IN REALITY, IT'S OUR BLOOD THEY'RE SUCKING...
ARE YOU LISTENING?
MMMM, YES, YES.
SOMEONE BROKE MY TAR.
WHO DID IT?
WHAT DIFFERENCE DOES IT MAKE?
DID YOU GO SEE MIRZA?
THAT OTHER CROOK!? WHATEVER...
HE TRIED TO CON ME FOUR TIMES. FOUR TARS, EACH ONE WORSE THAN THE OTHER.
I DON'T KNOW WHAT TO DO ANYMORE.
I THINK I HAVE A SOLUTION TO YOUR PROBLEM.

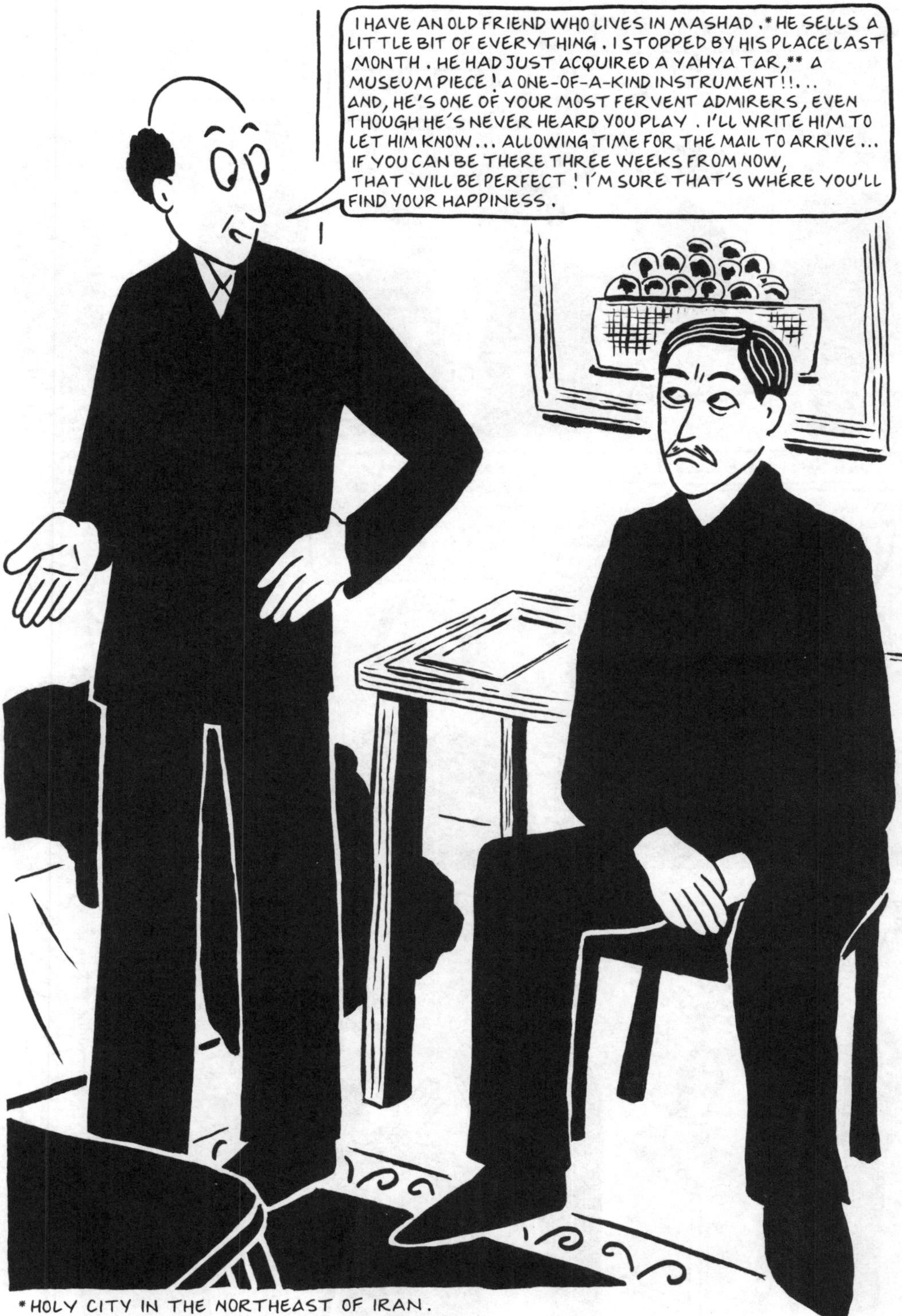
I HAVE AN OLD FRIEND WHO LIVES IN MASHAD.* HE SELLS A LITTLE BIT OF EVERYTHING. I STOPPED BY HIS PLACE LAST MONTH. HE HAD JUST ACQUIRED A YAHYA TAR,** A MUSEUM PIECE! A ONE-OF-A-KIND INSTRUMENT!!... AND, HE'S ONE OF YOUR MOST FERVENT ADMIRERS, EVEN THOUGH HE'S NEVER HEARD YOU PLAY. I'LL WRITE HIM TO LET HIM KNOW... ALLOWING TIME FOR THE MAIL TO ARRIVE... IF YOU CAN BE THERE THREE WEEKS FROM NOW, THAT WILL BE PERFECT! I'M SURE THAT'S WHERE YOU'LL FIND YOUR HAPPINESS.

*HOLY CITY IN THE NORTHEAST OF IRAN.

**THE EQUIVALENT OF A STRADIVARIUS VIOLIN.

18 DAYS LATER, NOVEMBER 10, 1958

I'M LEAVING FOR MASHAD IN TWO DAYS.

DID YOU HEAR WHAT I SAID?

I'M NOT DEAF LIKE YOUR MOTHER!

LEAVE THE DEAD WHERE THEY ARE.

I WORK ALL DAY. MINA, FARZANEH AND REZA GO TO SCHOOL, BUT HIM!

WHO WILL TAKE CARE OF HIM?

WELL, YOUR MOTHER, AS USUAL.

SHE'S NOT HERE THIS WEEK.

THAT'S NOT MY PROBLEM! IF YOU HADN'T BROKEN MY TAR, I WOULDN'T BE FORCED TO MAKE THIS TRIP!

YOU DIDN'T HAVE TO GET ON MY NERVES.

YOU DARE?

AND HOW!

BITCH!

BASTARD!

I'LL GO ALONE!! YOU HEAR?

ALONE!!!

10

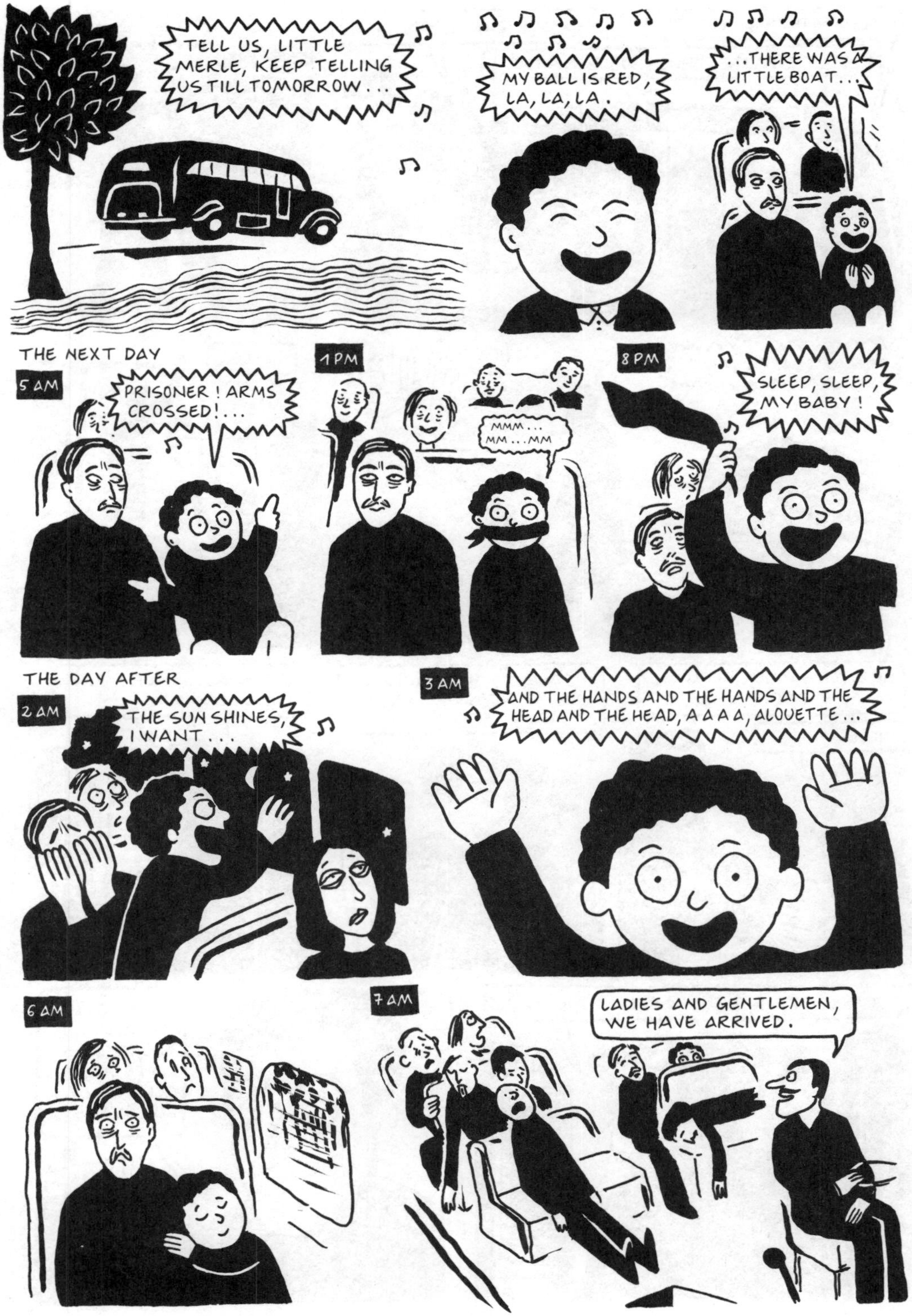
TELL US, LITTLE MERLE, KEEP TELLING US TILL TOMORROW...
MY BALL IS RED, LA, LA, LA.
...THERE WAS A LITTLE BOAT...
THE NEXT DAY
5 AM
PRISONER! ARMS CROSSED!...
1 PM
MMM... MM...MM
8 PM
SLEEP, SLEEP, MY BABY!
THE DAY AFTER
2 AM
THE SUN SHINES, I WANT...
3 AM
AND THE HANDS AND THE HANDS AND THE HEAD AND THE HEAD, A A A A, ALOUETTE...
6 AM
7 AM
LADIES AND GENTLEMEN, WE HAVE ARRIVED.

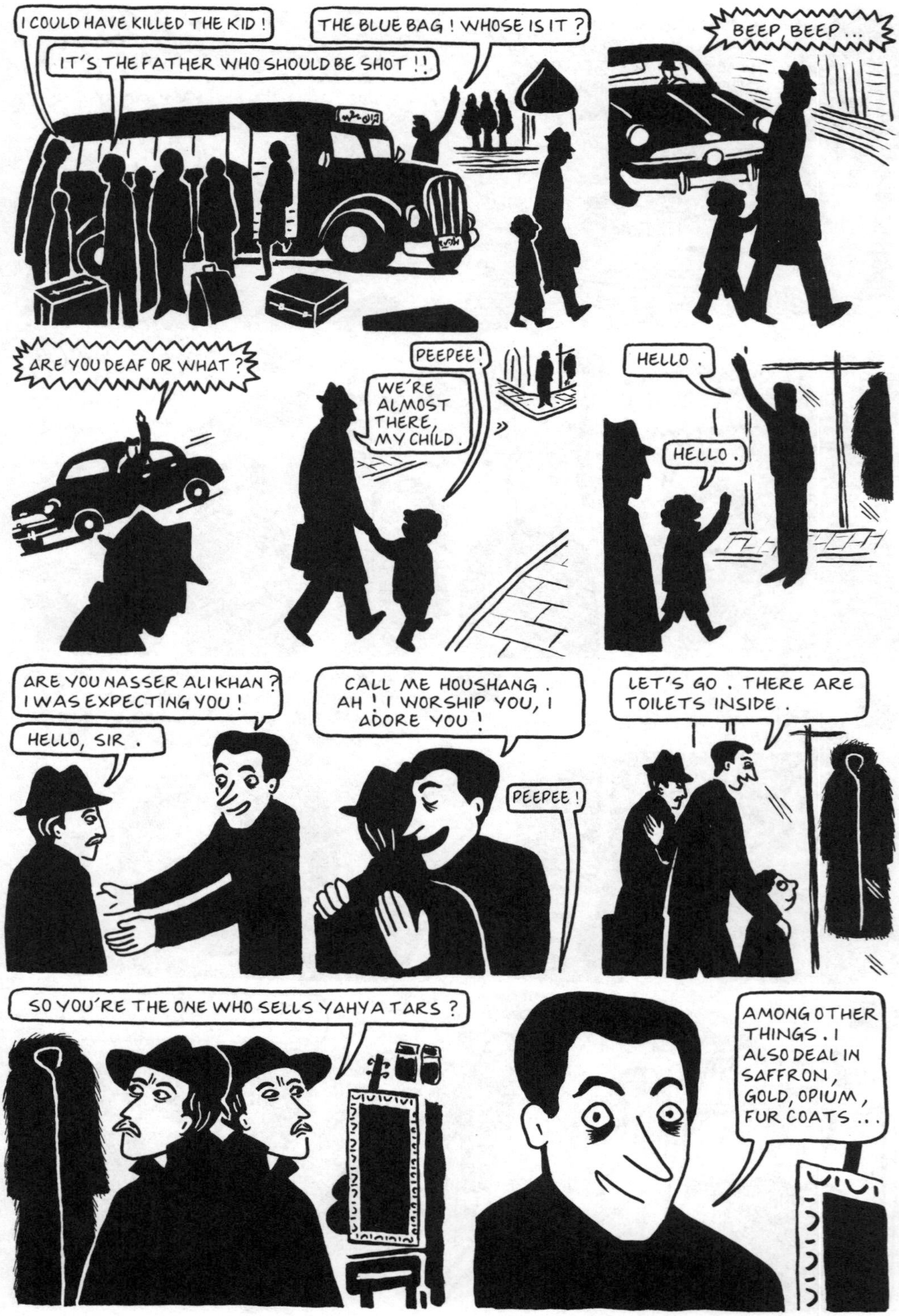
I COULD HAVE KILLED THE KID !
IT'S THE FATHER WHO SHOULD BE SHOT !!
THE BLUE BAG ! WHOSE IS IT ?
BEEP, BEEP...
ARE YOU DEAF OR WHAT ?
PEEPEE !
WE'RE ALMOST THERE, MY CHILD.
HELLO.
HELLO.
ARE YOU NASSER ALI KHAN ? I WAS EXPECTING YOU !
HELLO, SIR.
CALL ME HOUSHANG. AH ! I WORSHIP YOU, I ADORE YOU !
PEEPEE !
LET'S GO. THERE ARE TOILETS INSIDE.
SO YOU'RE THE ONE WHO SELLS YAHYA TARS ?
AMONG OTHER THINGS. I ALSO DEAL IN SAFFRON, GOLD, OPIUM, FUR COATS...

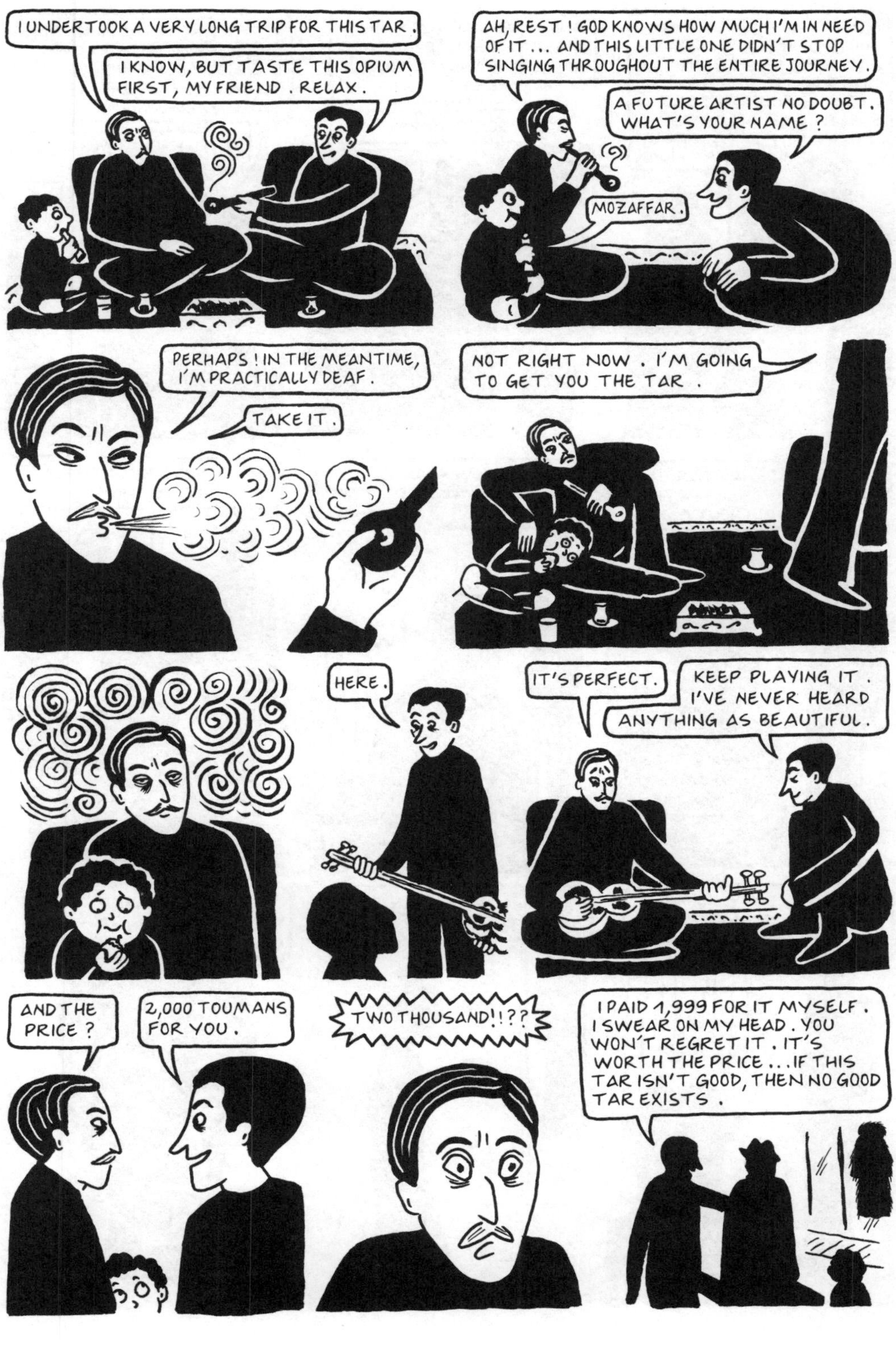
I UNDERTOOK A VERY LONG TRIP FOR THIS TAR.
I KNOW, BUT TASTE THIS OPIUM FIRST, MY FRIEND. RELAX.
AH, REST! GOD KNOWS HOW MUCH I'M IN NEED OF IT... AND THIS LITTLE ONE DIDN'T STOP SINGING THROUGHOUT THE ENTIRE JOURNEY.
A FUTURE ARTIST NO DOUBT. WHAT'S YOUR NAME?
MOZAFFAR.
PERHAPS! IN THE MEANTIME, I'M PRACTICALLY DEAF.
TAKE IT.
NOT RIGHT NOW. I'M GOING TO GET YOU THE TAR.
HERE.
IT'S PERFECT.
KEEP PLAYING IT. I'VE NEVER HEARD ANYTHING AS BEAUTIFUL.
AND THE PRICE?
2,000 TOUMANS FOR YOU.
TWO THOUSAND!!??
I PAID 1,999 FOR IT MYSELF. I SWEAR ON MY HEAD. YOU WON'T REGRET IT. IT'S WORTH THE PRICE... IF THIS TAR ISN'T GOOD, THEN NO GOOD TAR EXISTS.

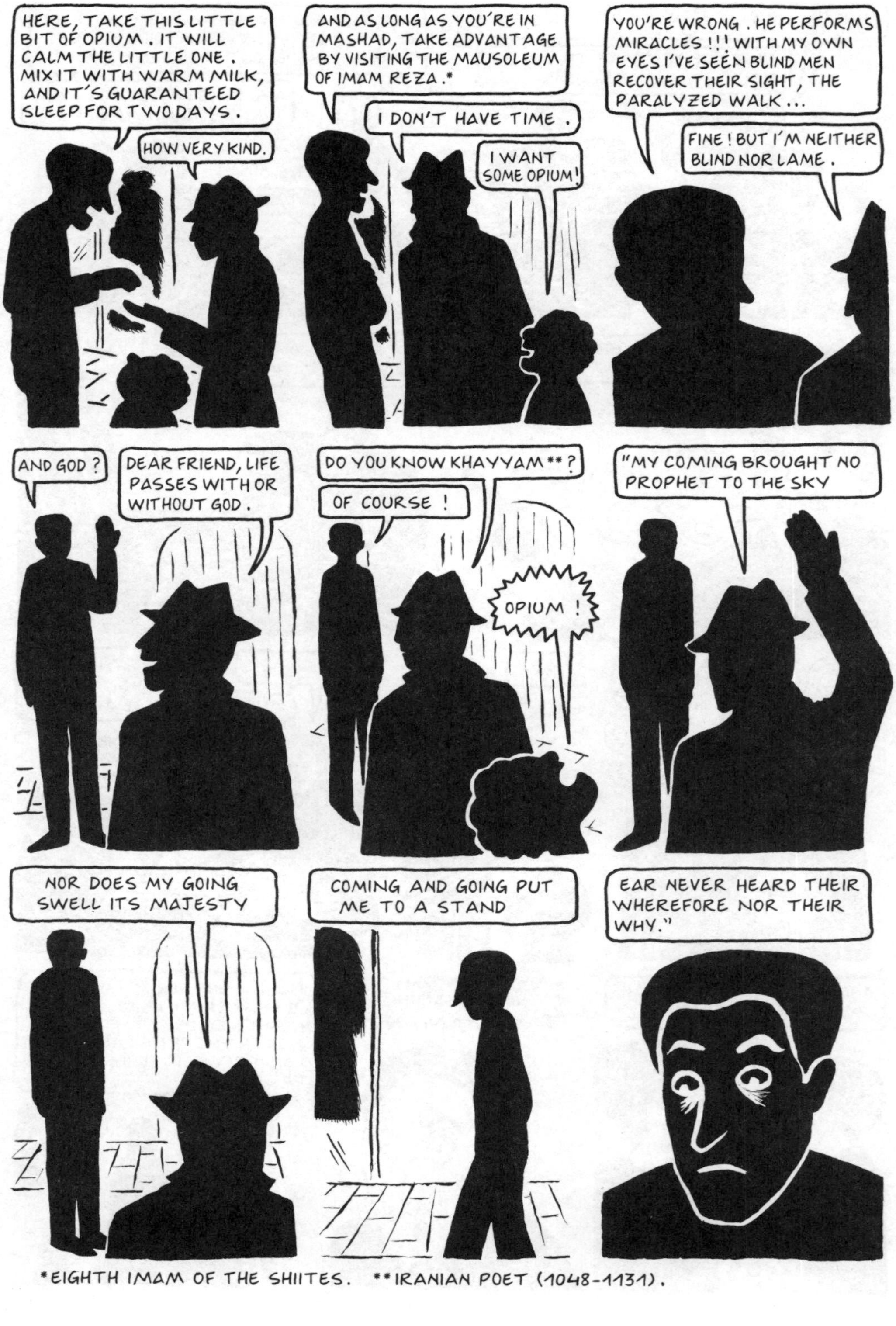
HERE, TAKE THIS LITTLE BIT OF OPIUM. IT WILL CALM THE LITTLE ONE. MIX IT WITH WARM MILK, AND IT'S GUARANTEED SLEEP FOR TWO DAYS.
HOW VERY KIND.
AND AS LONG AS YOU'RE IN MASHAD, TAKE ADVANTAGE BY VISITING THE MAUSOLEUM OF IMAM REZA.*
I DON'T HAVE TIME.
I WANT SOME OPIUM!
YOU'RE WRONG. HE PERFORMS MIRACLES!!! WITH MY OWN EYES I'VE SEEN BLIND MEN RECOVER THEIR SIGHT, THE PARALYZED WALK...
FINE! BUT I'M NEITHER BLIND NOR LAME.
AND GOD?
DEAR FRIEND, LIFE PASSES WITH OR WITHOUT GOD.
DO YOU KNOW KHAYYAM**?
OF COURSE!
OPIUM!
"MY COMING BROUGHT NO PROPHET TO THE SKY
NOR DOES MY GOING SWELL ITS MAJESTY
COMING AND GOING PUT ME TO A STAND
EAR NEVER HEARD THEIR WHEREFORE NOR THEIR WHY."

*EIGHTH IMAM OF THE SHIITES. **IRANIAN POET (1048-1131).

THEY LEFT THAT VERY NIGHT...

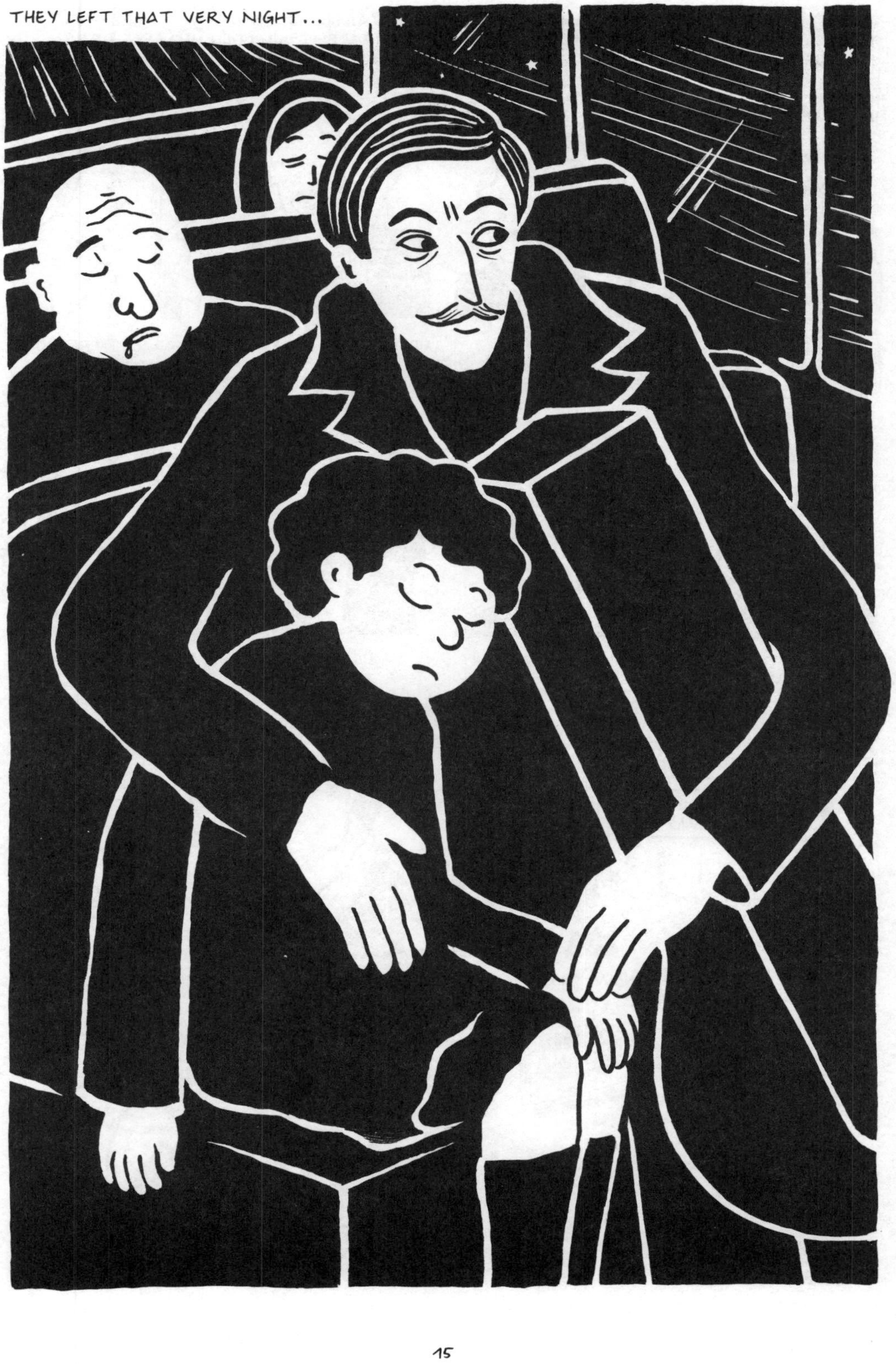

...AND ARRIVED TWO NIGHTS LATER IN TEHRAN. NASSER ALI KHAN PUT MOZAFFAR TO BED. HE HAD ONLY ONE DESIRE: TO PLAY HIS TAR. BUT HE TOLD HIMSELF HE SHOULD WAIT UNTIL MORNING.

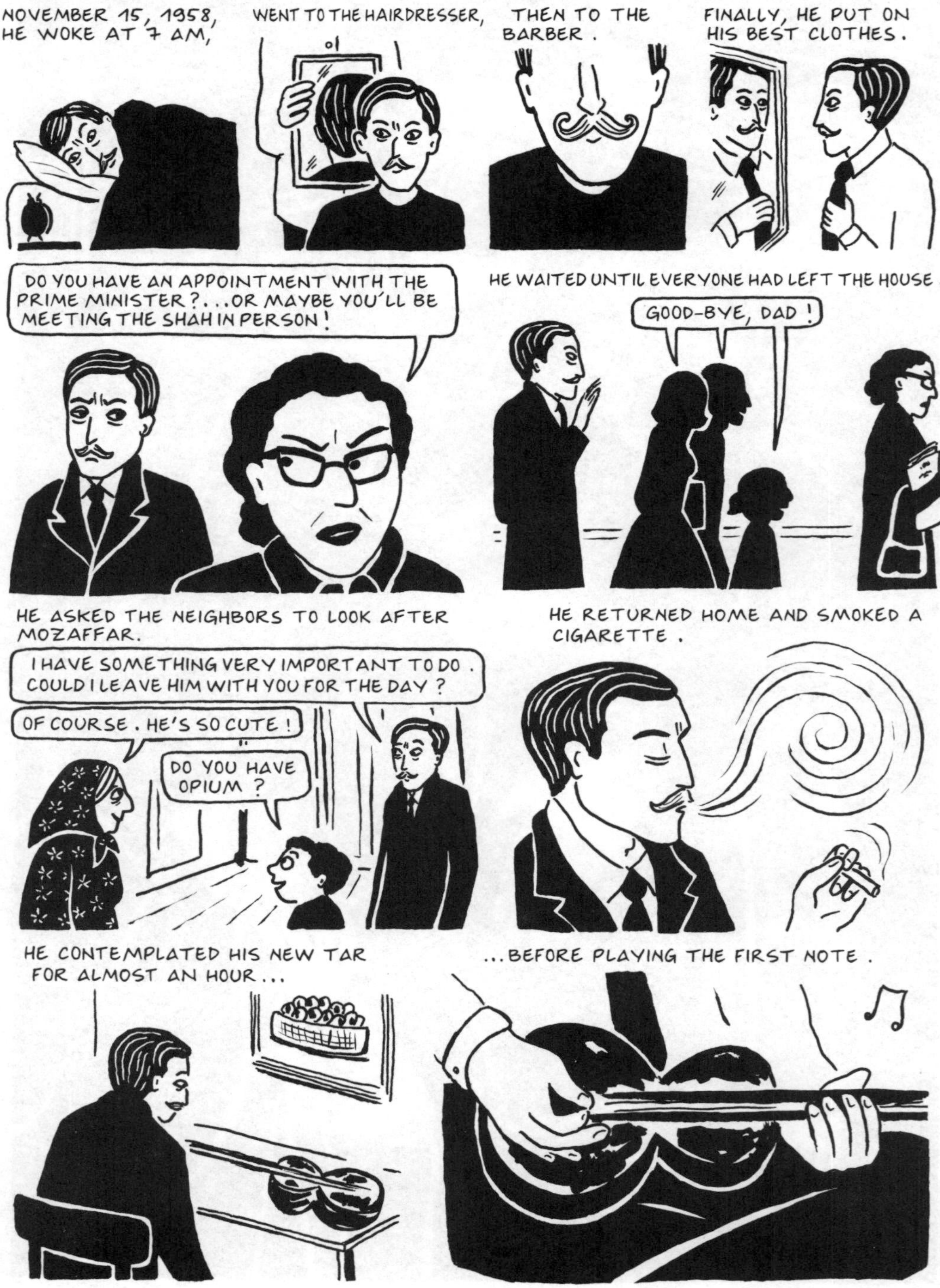

NOVEMBER 15, 1958, HE WOKE AT 7 AM,
WENT TO THE HAIRDRESSER,
THEN TO THE BARBER.
FINALLY, HE PUT ON HIS BEST CLOTHES.
DO YOU HAVE AN APPOINTMENT WITH THE PRIME MINISTER?...OR MAYBE YOU'LL BE MEETING THE SHAH IN PERSON!
HE WAITED UNTIL EVERYONE HAD LEFT THE HOUSE.
GOOD-BYE, DAD!
HE ASKED THE NEIGHBORS TO LOOK AFTER MOZAFFAR.
I HAVE SOMETHING VERY IMPORTANT TO DO. COULD I LEAVE HIM WITH YOU FOR THE DAY?
OF COURSE. HE'S SO CUTE!
DO YOU HAVE OPIUM?
HE RETURNED HOME AND SMOKED A CIGARETTE.
HE CONTEMPLATED HIS NEW TAR FOR ALMOST AN HOUR...
...BEFORE PLAYING THE FIRST NOTE.

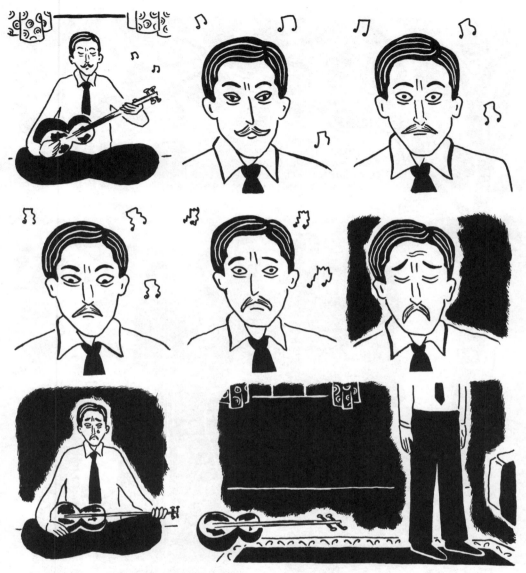

SINCE NO OTHER TAR COULD GIVE HIM THE PLEASURE OF PLAYING, NASSER ALI KHAN DECIDED TO DIE. HE LAY DOWN IN HIS BED...

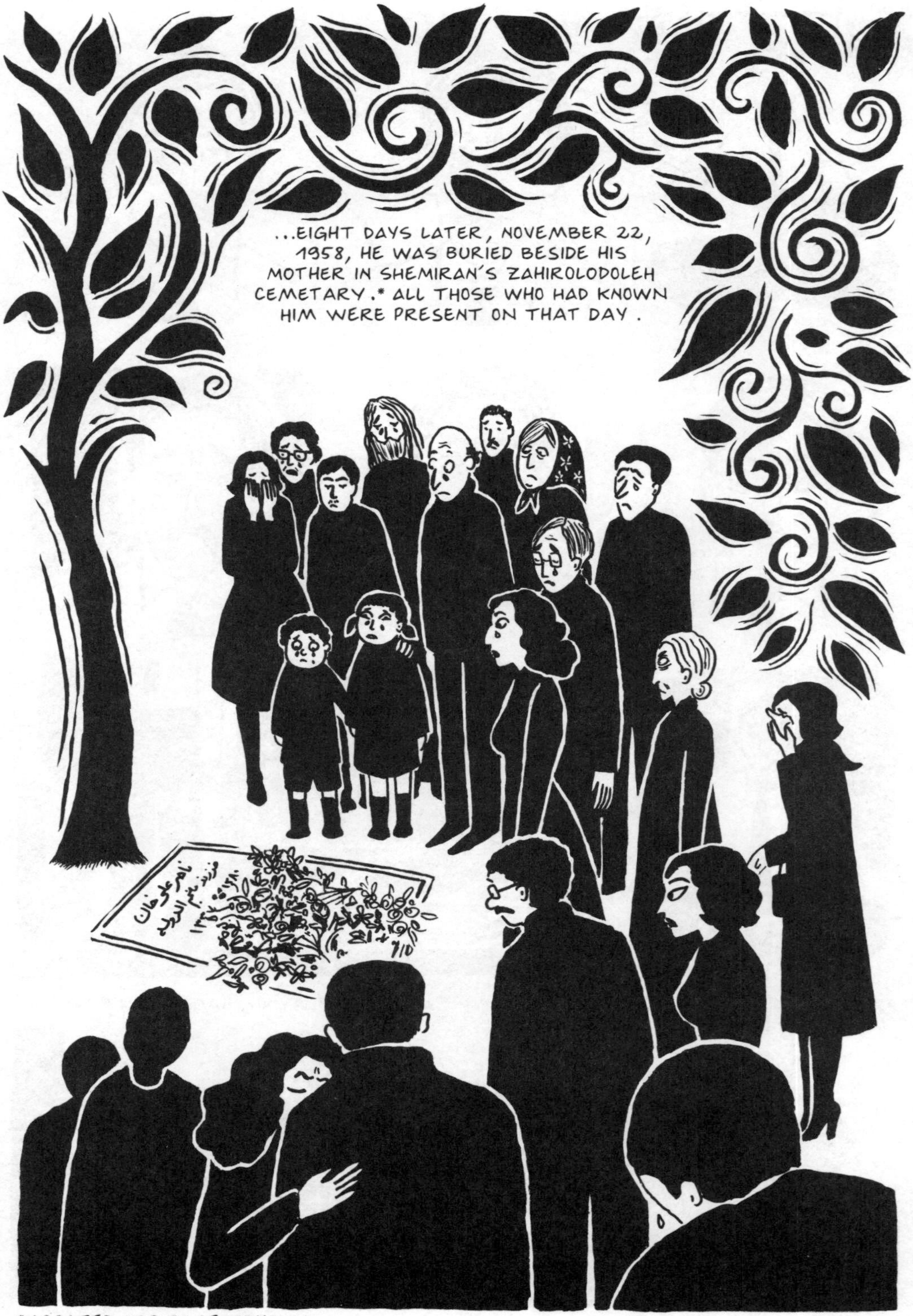
...EIGHT DAYS LATER, NOVEMBER 22, 1958, HE WAS BURIED BESIDE HIS MOTHER IN SHEMIRAN'S ZAHIROLODOLEH CEMETARY.* ALL THOSE WHO HAD KNOWN HIM WERE PRESENT ON THAT DAY.

* LOCATED NORTH OF TEHRAN.

THE FIRST DAY

NOVEMBER 15, 1958

NOVEMBER 15, 1958 . NASSER ALI KHAN MADE UP HIS MIND TO SURRENDER HIS SOUL . HE CONSIDERED THE DIFFERENT WAYS TO PUT AN END TO HIS DAYS .

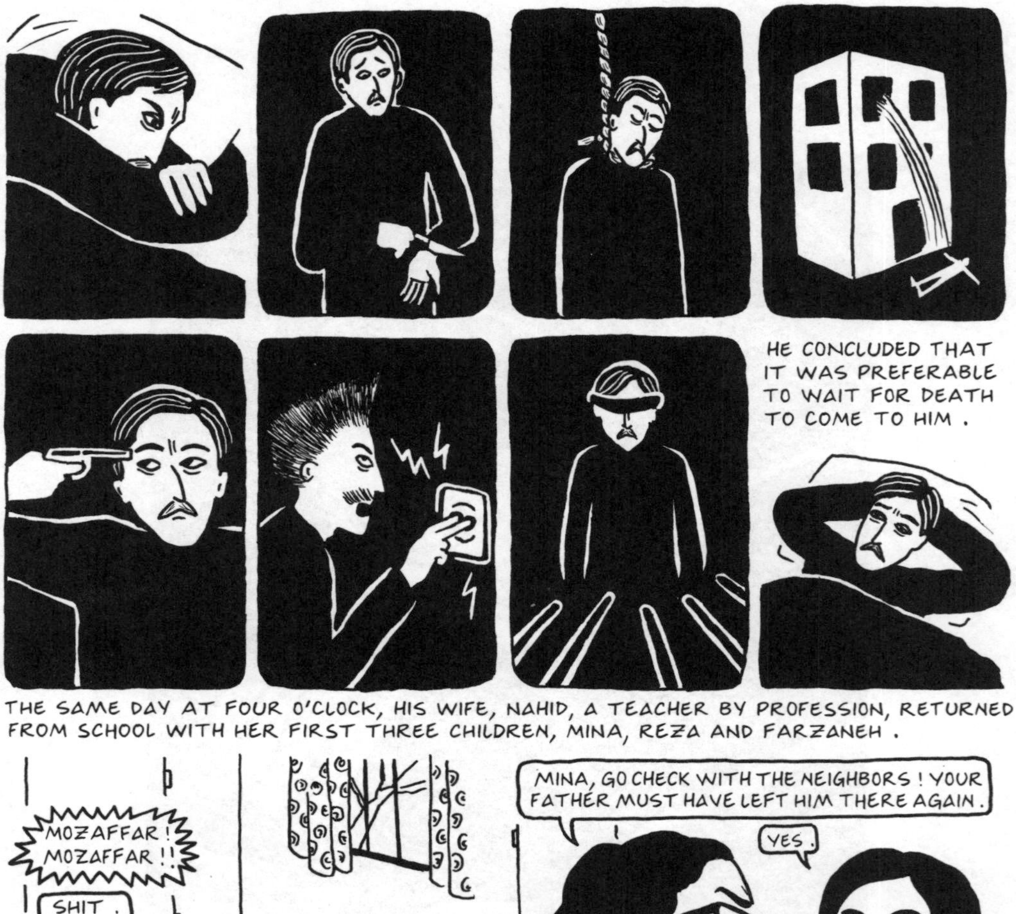
HE CONCLUDED THAT IT WAS PREFERABLE TO WAIT FOR DEATH TO COME TO HIM .

THE SAME DAY AT FOUR O'CLOCK, HIS WIFE, NAHID, A TEACHER BY PROFESSION, RETURNED FROM SCHOOL WITH HER FIRST THREE CHILDREN, MINA, REZA AND FARZANEH .

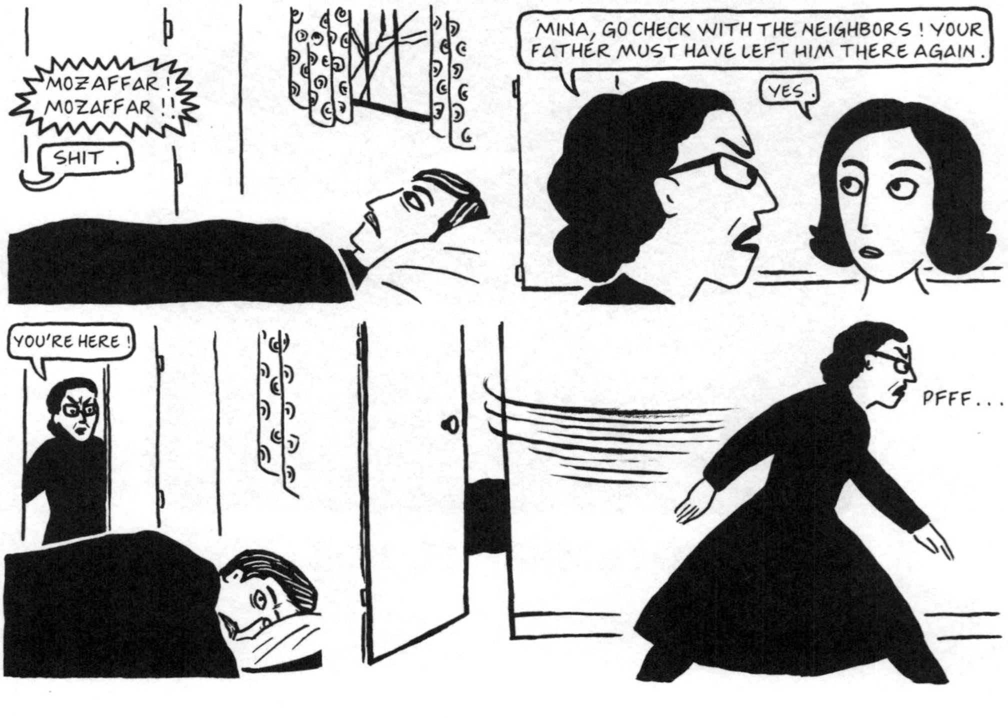
MOZAFFAR ! MOZAFFAR !!
SHIT .
MINA, GO CHECK WITH THE NEIGHBORS ! YOUR FATHER MUST HAVE LEFT HIM THERE AGAIN .
YES .
YOU'RE HERE !
PFFF...

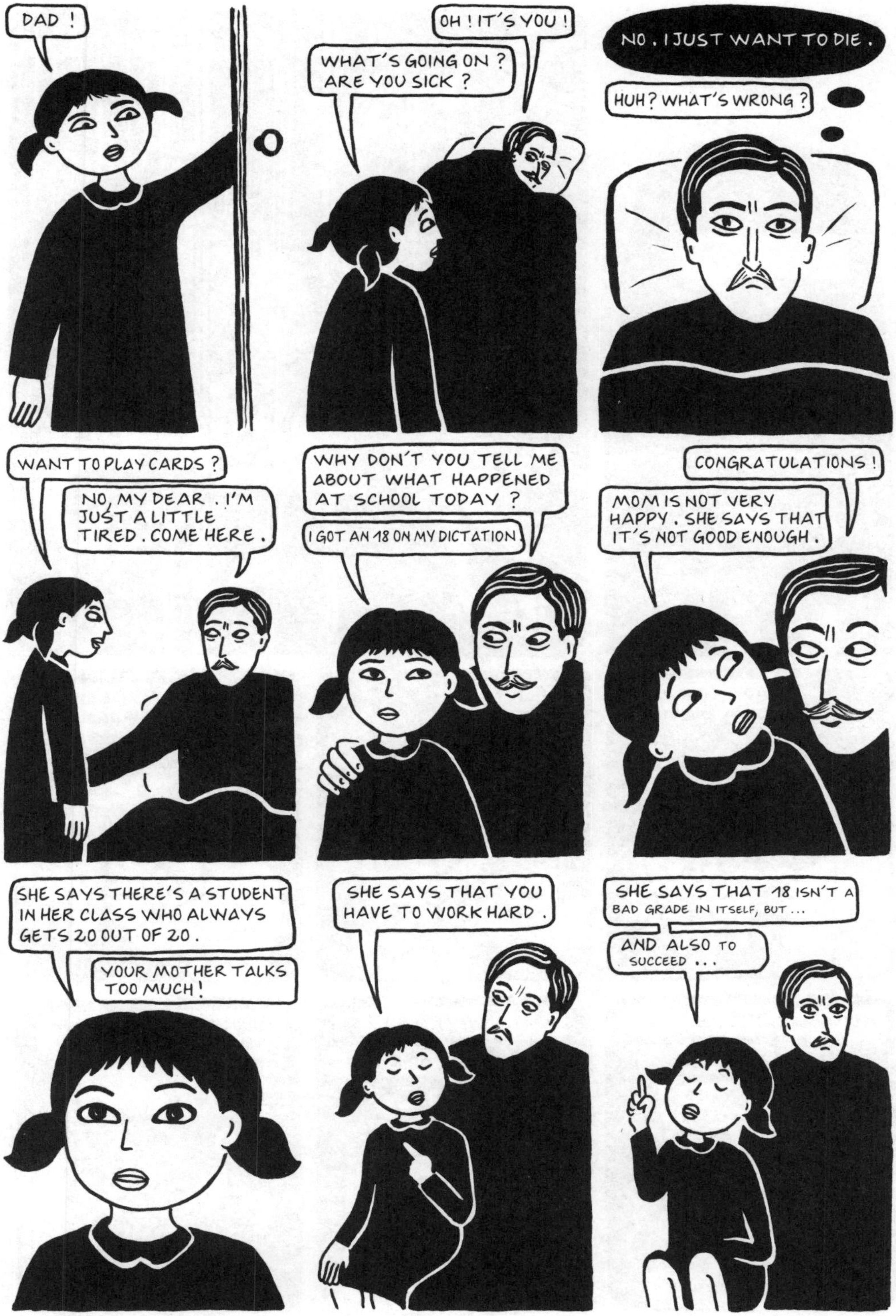
DAD !
OH ! IT'S YOU !
WHAT'S GOING ON ? ARE YOU SICK ?
NO. I JUST WANT TO DIE.
HUH? WHAT'S WRONG ?
WANT TO PLAY CARDS ?
NO, MY DEAR. I'M JUST A LITTLE TIRED. COME HERE.
WHY DON'T YOU TELL ME ABOUT WHAT HAPPENED AT SCHOOL TODAY ?
I GOT AN 18 ON MY DICTATION.
CONGRATULATIONS !
MOM IS NOT VERY HAPPY. SHE SAYS THAT IT'S NOT GOOD ENOUGH.
SHE SAYS THERE'S A STUDENT IN HER CLASS WHO ALWAYS GETS 20 OUT OF 20.
YOUR MOTHER TALKS TOO MUCH!
SHE SAYS THAT YOU HAVE TO WORK HARD.
SHE SAYS THAT 18 ISN'T A BAD GRADE IN ITSELF, BUT ...
AND ALSO TO SUCCEED ...

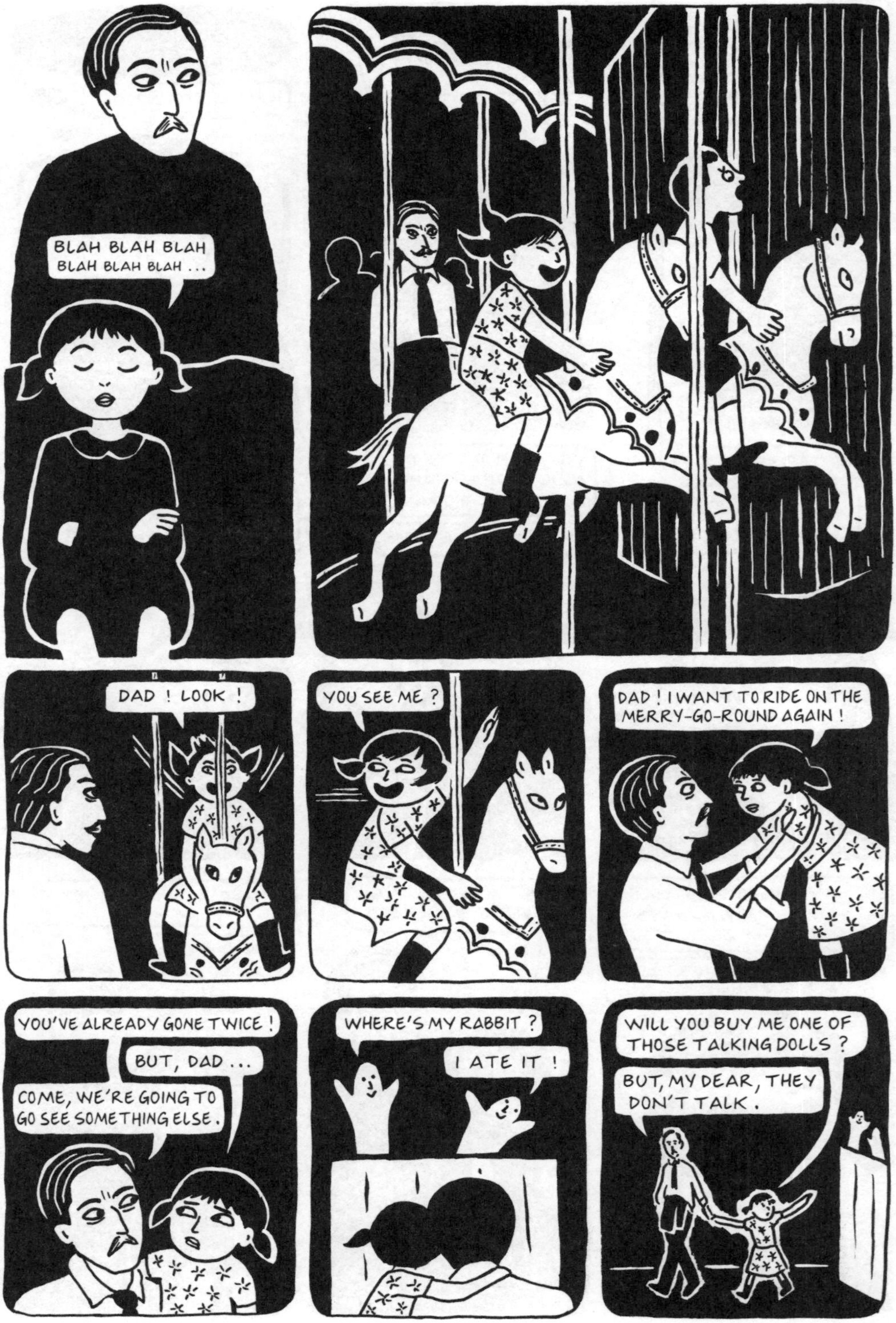
BLAH BLAH BLAH
BLAH BLAH BLAH ...
DAD ! LOOK !
YOU SEE ME ?
DAD ! I WANT TO RIDE ON THE MERRY-GO-ROUND AGAIN !
YOU'VE ALREADY GONE TWICE !
BUT, DAD ...
COME, WE'RE GOING TO GO SEE SOMETHING ELSE .
WHERE'S MY RABBIT ?
I ATE IT !
WILL YOU BUY ME ONE OF THOSE TALKING DOLLS ?
BUT, MY DEAR, THEY DON'T TALK .

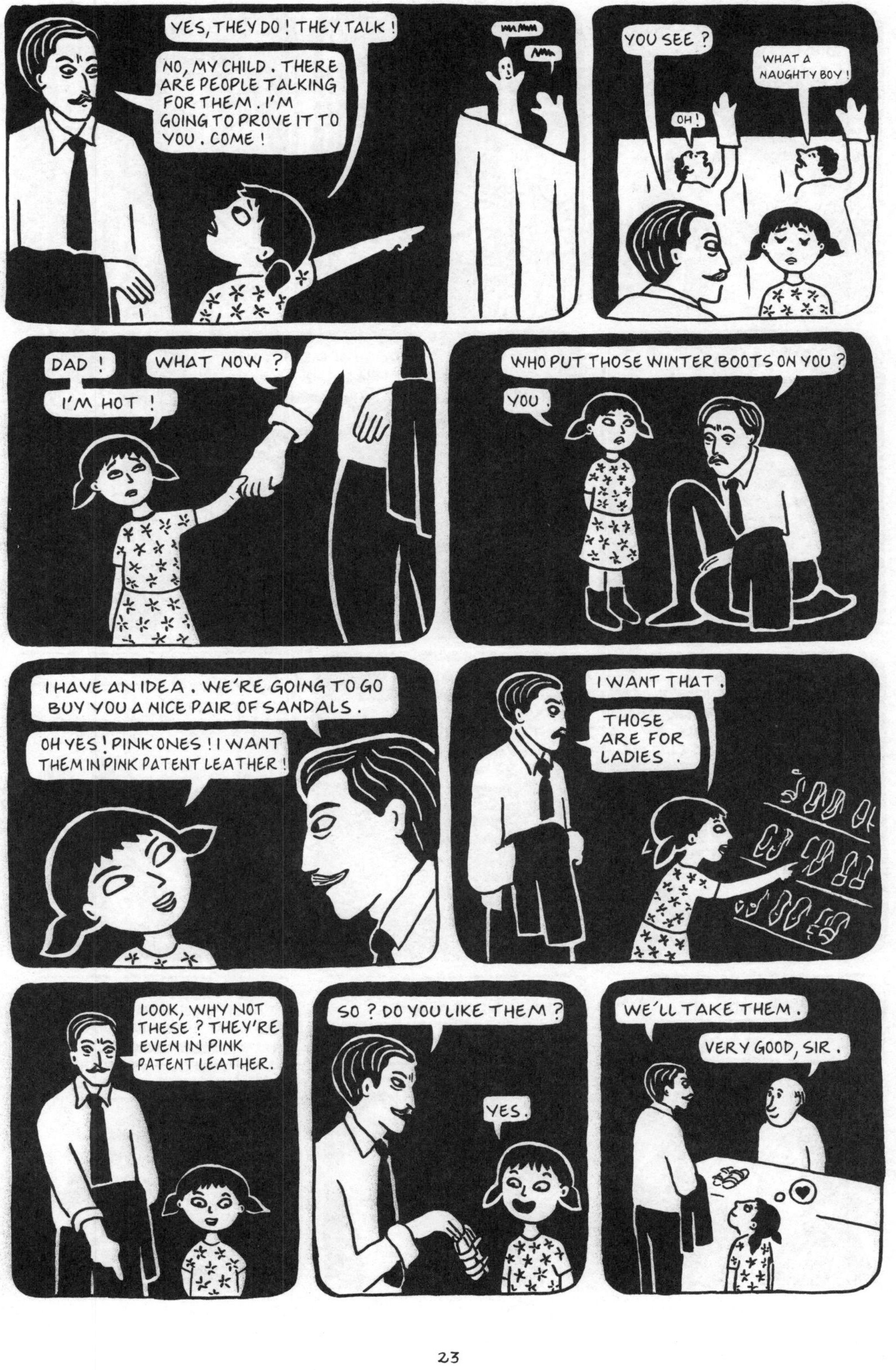
YES, THEY DO! THEY TALK!
NO, MY CHILD. THERE ARE PEOPLE TALKING FOR THEM. I'M GOING TO PROVE IT TO YOU. COME!
YOU SEE?
OH!
WHAT A NAUGHTY BOY!
DAD!
WHAT NOW?
I'M HOT!
WHO PUT THOSE WINTER BOOTS ON YOU?
YOU.
I HAVE AN IDEA. WE'RE GOING TO GO BUY YOU A NICE PAIR OF SANDALS.
OH YES! PINK ONES! I WANT THEM IN PINK PATENT LEATHER!
I WANT THAT.
THOSE ARE FOR LADIES.
LOOK, WHY NOT THESE? THEY'RE EVEN IN PINK PATENT LEATHER.
SO? DO YOU LIKE THEM?
YES.
WE'LL TAKE THEM.
VERY GOOD, SIR.

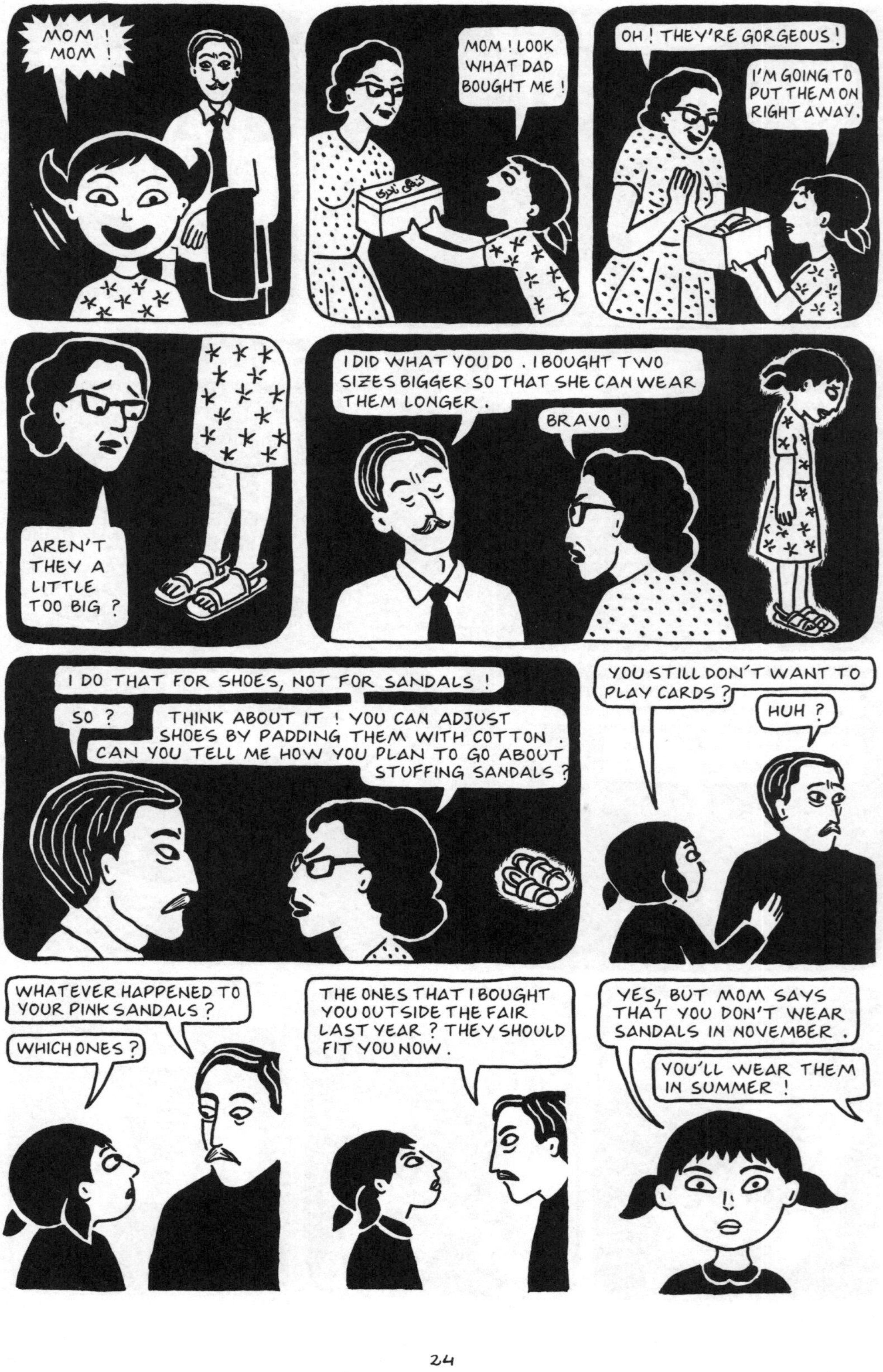
MOM ! MOM !
MOM ! LOOK WHAT DAD BOUGHT ME !
OH ! THEY'RE GORGEOUS !
I'M GOING TO PUT THEM ON RIGHT AWAY.
AREN'T THEY A LITTLE TOO BIG ?
I DID WHAT YOU DO . I BOUGHT TWO SIZES BIGGER SO THAT SHE CAN WEAR THEM LONGER .
BRAVO !
I DO THAT FOR SHOES, NOT FOR SANDALS !
SO ?
THINK ABOUT IT ! YOU CAN ADJUST SHOES BY PADDING THEM WITH COTTON . CAN YOU TELL ME HOW YOU PLAN TO GO ABOUT STUFFING SANDALS ?
YOU STILL DON'T WANT TO PLAY CARDS ?
HUH ?
WHATEVER HAPPENED TO YOUR PINK SANDALS ?
WHICH ONES ?
THE ONES THAT I BOUGHT YOU OUTSIDE THE FAIR LAST YEAR ? THEY SHOULD FIT YOU NOW .
YES, BUT MOM SAYS THAT YOU DON'T WEAR SANDALS IN NOVEMBER .
YOU'LL WEAR THEM IN SUMMER !

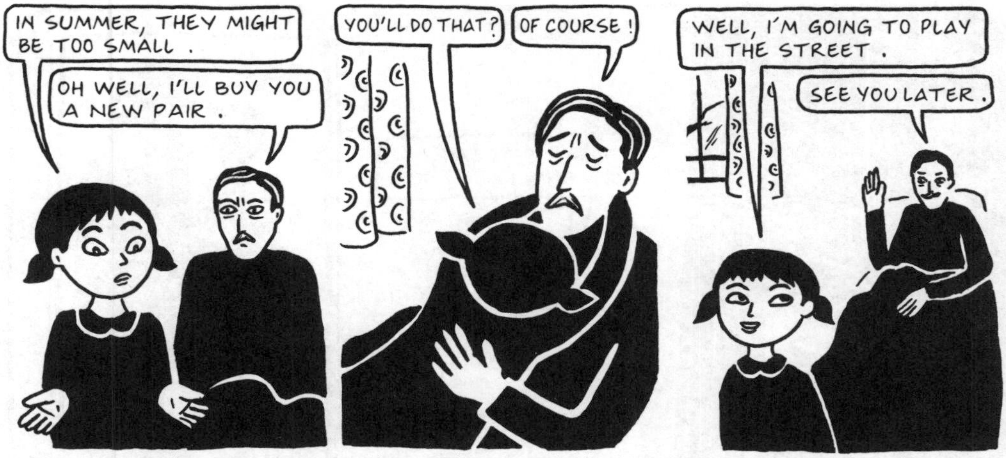
IN SUMMER, THEY MIGHT BE TOO SMALL.
OH WELL, I'LL BUY YOU A NEW PAIR.
YOU'LL DO THAT?
OF COURSE!
WELL, I'M GOING TO PLAY IN THE STREET.
SEE YOU LATER.

OF HIS FOUR CHILDREN, FARZANEH WAS HER FATHER'S FAVORITE. POSSESSED BY AN UNUSUAL INTEREST IN MORPHOPSYCHOLOGY, NASSER ALI KHAN WAS CONVINCED THAT HIS PHYSICAL RESEMBLANCE TO HIS YOUNGEST DAUGHTER PROVED THE CLOSENESS OF THEIR SOULS. AND HE WASN'T WRONG. THEY WERE BOTH VERY INTELLIGENT, LIVELY AND SPIRITUAL BEINGS. I REMEMBER IN 1998, DURING ONE OF MY VISITS TO TEHRAN...

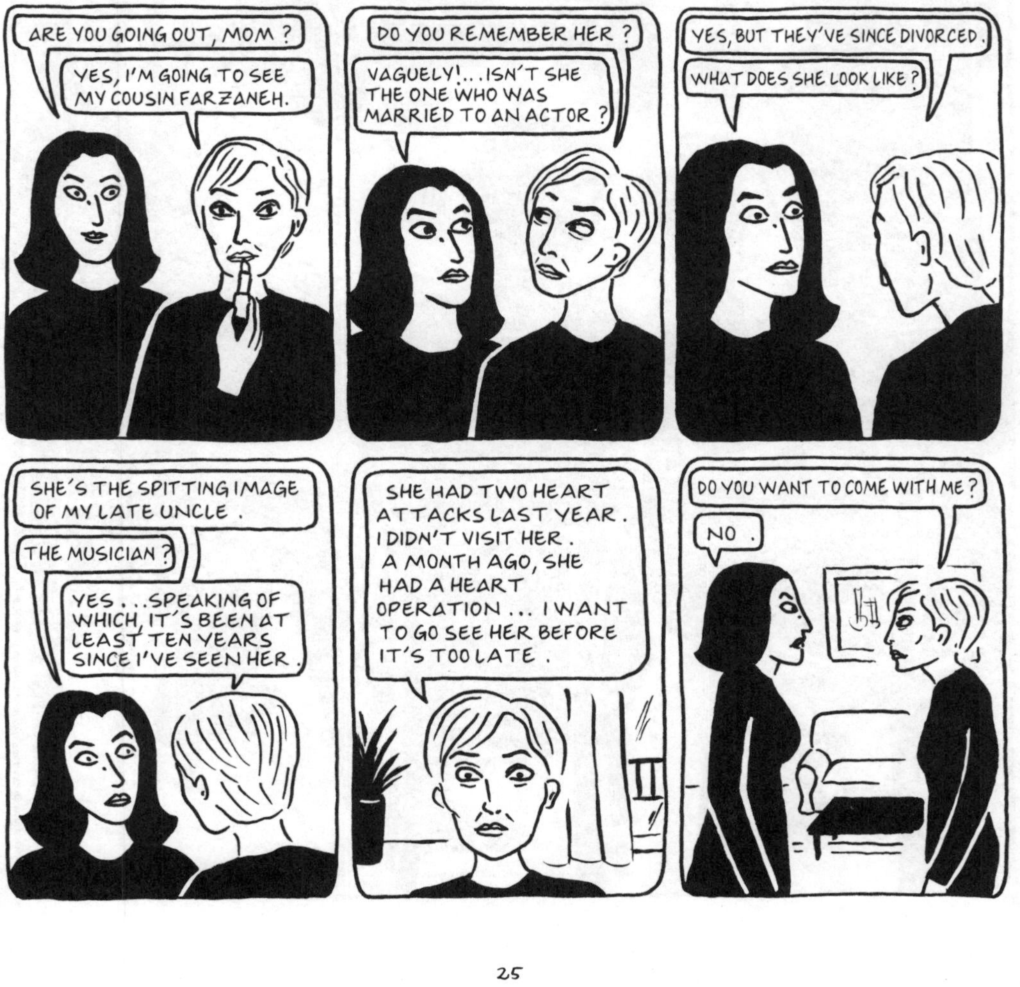
ARE YOU GOING OUT, MOM?
YES, I'M GOING TO SEE MY COUSIN FARZANEH.
DO YOU REMEMBER HER?
VAGUELY!... ISN'T SHE THE ONE WHO WAS MARRIED TO AN ACTOR?
YES, BUT THEY'VE SINCE DIVORCED.
WHAT DOES SHE LOOK LIKE?
SHE'S THE SPITTING IMAGE OF MY LATE UNCLE.
THE MUSICIAN?
YES... SPEAKING OF WHICH, IT'S BEEN AT LEAST TEN YEARS SINCE I'VE SEEN HER.
SHE HAD TWO HEART ATTACKS LAST YEAR. I DIDN'T VISIT HER. A MONTH AGO, SHE HAD A HEART OPERATION... I WANT TO GO SEE HER BEFORE IT'S TOO LATE.
DO YOU WANT TO COME WITH ME?
NO.

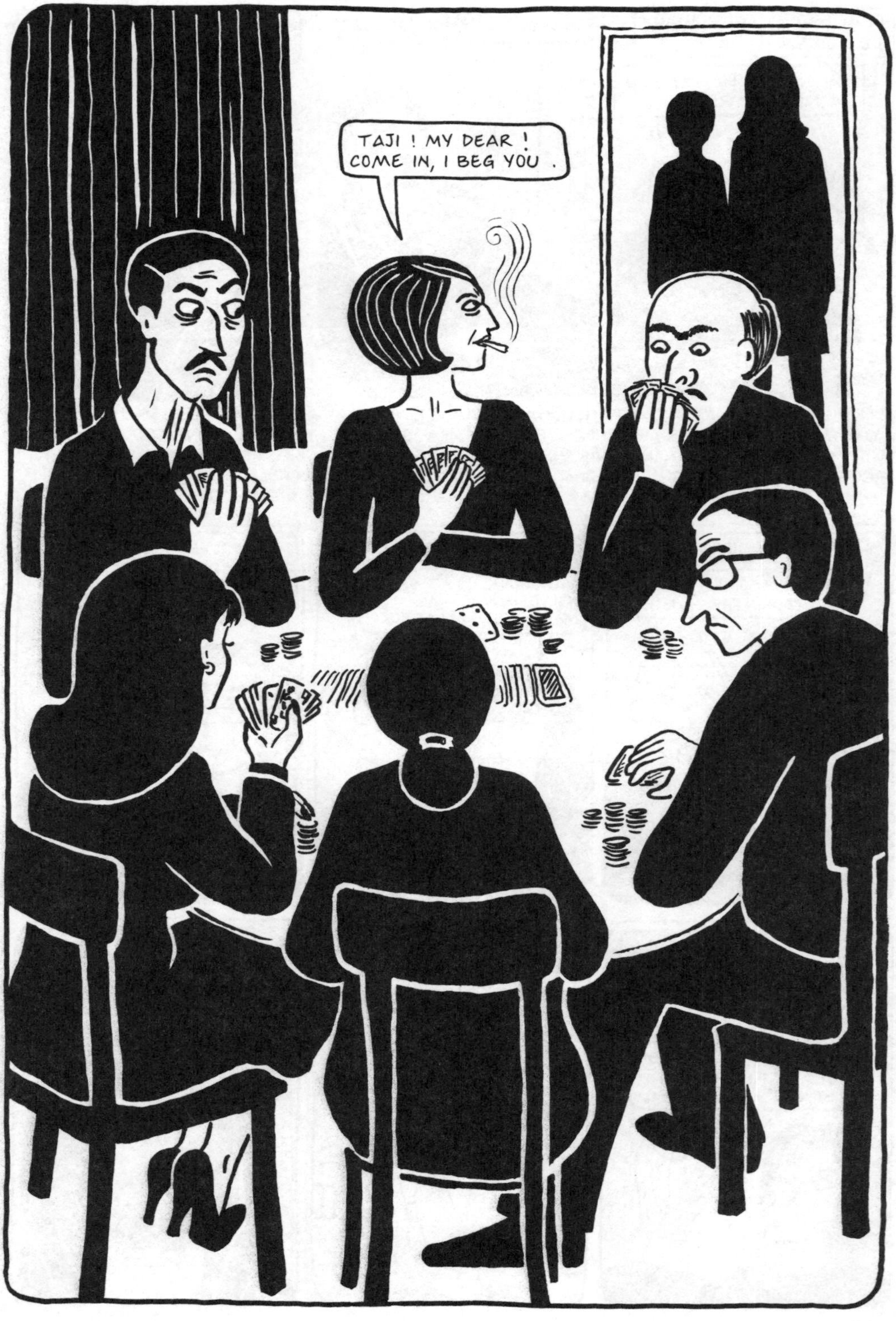
TAJI ! MY DEAR ! COME IN, I BEG YOU .

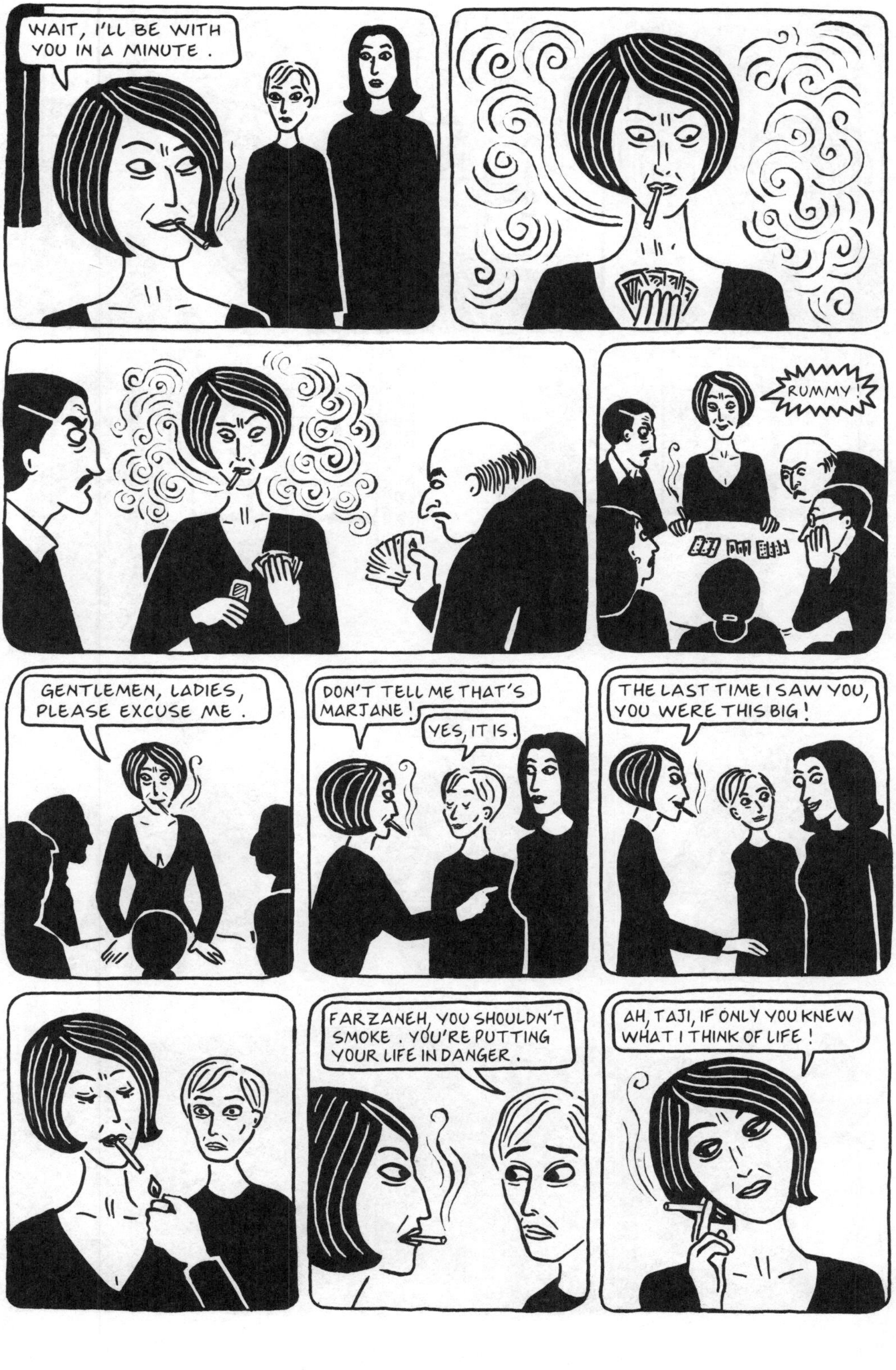
WAIT, I'LL BE WITH YOU IN A MINUTE.
RUMMY!
GENTLEMEN, LADIES, PLEASE EXCUSE ME.
DON'T TELL ME THAT'S MARJANE!
YES, IT IS.
THE LAST TIME I SAW YOU, YOU WERE THIS BIG!
FARZANEH, YOU SHOULDN'T SMOKE. YOU'RE PUTTING YOUR LIFE IN DANGER.
AH, TAJI, IF ONLY YOU KNEW WHAT I THINK OF LIFE!

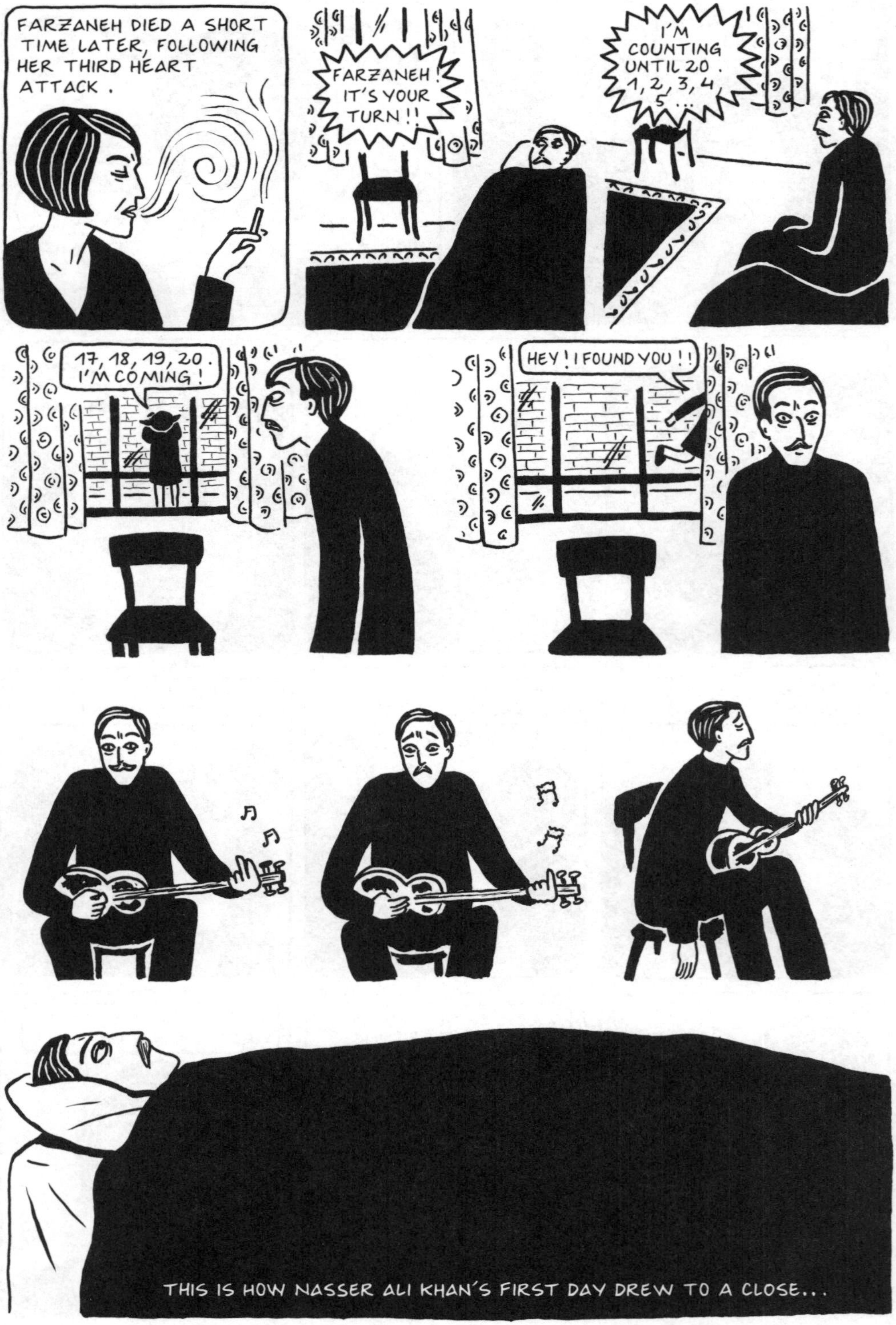
FARZANEH DIED A SHORT TIME LATER, FOLLOWING HER THIRD HEART ATTACK.
FARZANEH! IT'S YOUR TURN!!
I'M COUNTING UNTIL 20. 1, 2, 3, 4, 5...
17, 18, 19, 20. I'M COMING!
HEY! I FOUND YOU!!
THIS IS HOW NASSER ALI KHAN'S FIRST DAY DREW TO A CLOSE...

THE SECOND DAY

NOVEMBER 16, 1958

THE SECOND DAY FELL ON A FRIDAY. AT 12:30, NASSER ALI KHAN'S WIFE, NAHID, REALIZED THAT HER HUSBAND STILL HADN'T EMERGED FROM THE BEDROOM. SHE WAS WORRIED, BUT GIVEN THE DAMAGED STATE OF THEIR RELATIONSHIP, SHE DECIDED THAT SHE'D BE BETTER OFF CONSULTING ABDI, HER HUSBAND'S BROTHER.

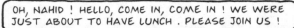

OH, NAHID! HELLO, COME IN, COME IN! WE WERE JUST ABOUT TO HAVE LUNCH. PLEASE JOIN US!

NO THANKS, I DON'T WANT TO DISTURB YOU.

ON THE CONTRARY, WE'D BE HONORED BY YOUR PRESENCE!

NO, REALLY... MY CHILDREN ARE WAITING FOR ME.

I CAME TO TALK TO YOU ABOUT NASSER ALI.

WHAT ABOUT NASSER ALI? HAS SOMETHING HAPPENED TO HIM?

NOT EXACTLY... HE HASN'T COME OUT OF HIS ROOM FOR TWO DAYS.

HE MUST BE IN A CREATIVE STATE...

YOU KNOW ARTISTS... WHEN INSPIRATION STRIKES, IT STRIKES!... I SEE HIM... IN PERFECT HARMONY WITH HIS TAR!

HE DOESN'T HAVE A TAR ANYMORE I MEAN, HE HAS ONE BUT NOT THE ONE YOU'RE THINKING OF.

HE HAS A NEW ONE. HE BOUGHT IT FROM MASHAD...

WAIT! WHERE IS "HIS" TAR?

...I BROKE IT.

HUNH?...BUT...YOU HAD NO RIGHT!

AND WHAT ABOUT HIM? DID HE HAVE THE RIGHT TO INSULT ME?

PLEASE! THAT'S NOT A REASON!

HE DOESN'T GO OUT ANY-MORE, HE DOESN'T EAT...

COME ON, COME ON, ALL COUPLES FIGHT, IT WILL WORK ITSELF OUT.

ABDI! PLEASE! HELP ME! DO SOMETHING!!

COLLECT YOURSELF. I'LL COME BY IN A LITTLE WHILE.

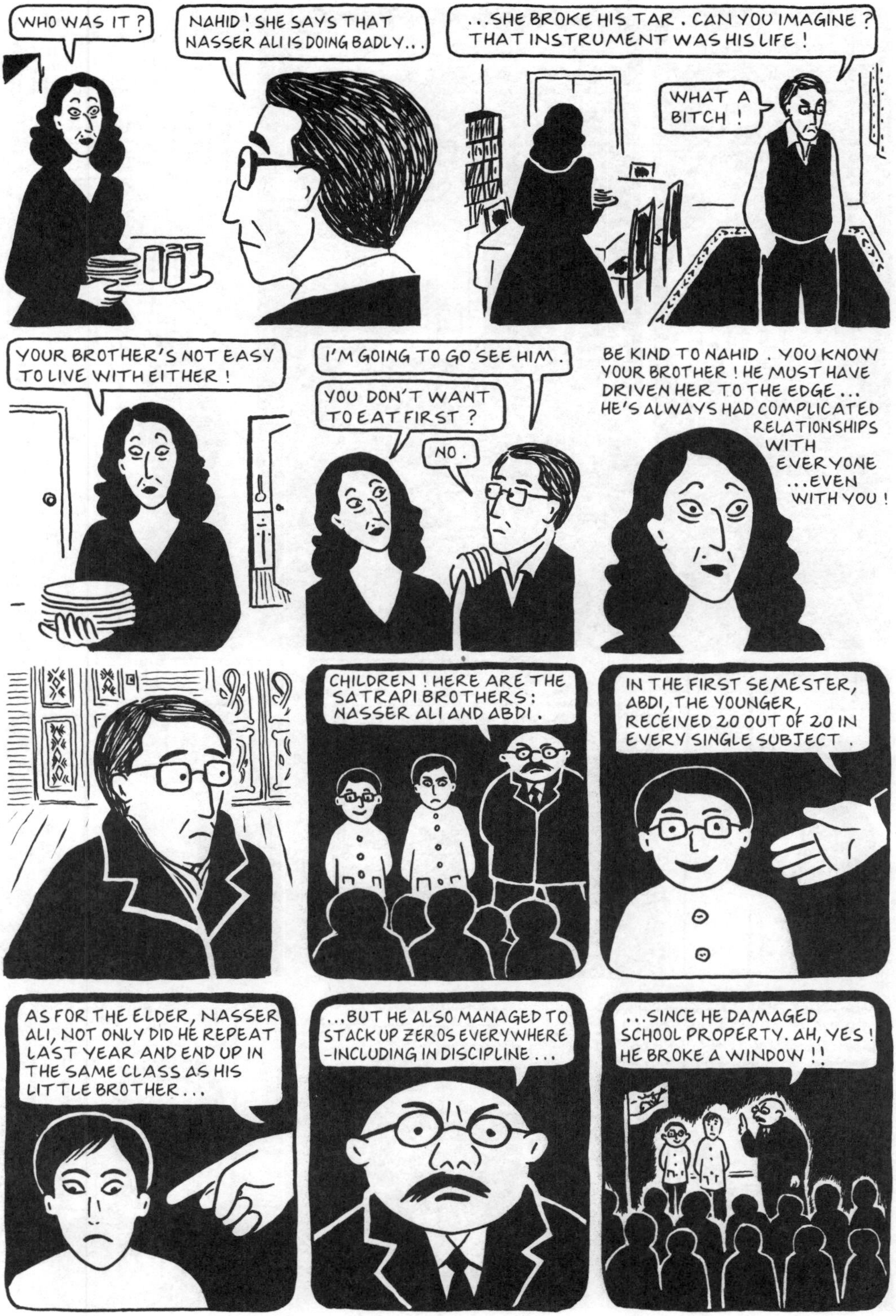
WHO WAS IT ?
NAHID ! SHE SAYS THAT NASSER ALI IS DOING BADLY . . .
. . . SHE BROKE HIS TAR . CAN YOU IMAGINE ? THAT INSTRUMENT WAS HIS LIFE !
WHAT A BITCH !
YOUR BROTHER'S NOT EASY TO LIVE WITH EITHER !
I'M GOING TO GO SEE HIM .
YOU DON'T WANT TO EAT FIRST ?
NO .
BE KIND TO NAHID . YOU KNOW YOUR BROTHER ! HE MUST HAVE DRIVEN HER TO THE EDGE . . . HE'S ALWAYS HAD COMPLICATED RELATIONSHIPS WITH EVERYONE . . . EVEN WITH YOU !
CHILDREN ! HERE ARE THE SATRAPI BROTHERS : NASSER ALI AND ABDI .
IN THE FIRST SEMESTER, ABDI, THE YOUNGER, RECEIVED 20 OUT OF 20 IN EVERY SINGLE SUBJECT .
AS FOR THE ELDER, NASSER ALI, NOT ONLY DID HE REPEAT LAST YEAR AND END UP IN THE SAME CLASS AS HIS LITTLE BROTHER . . .
. . . BUT HE ALSO MANAGED TO STACK UP ZEROS EVERYWHERE -INCLUDING IN DISCIPLINE . . .
. . . SINCE HE DAMAGED SCHOOL PROPERTY. AH, YES ! HE BROKE A WINDOW ! !

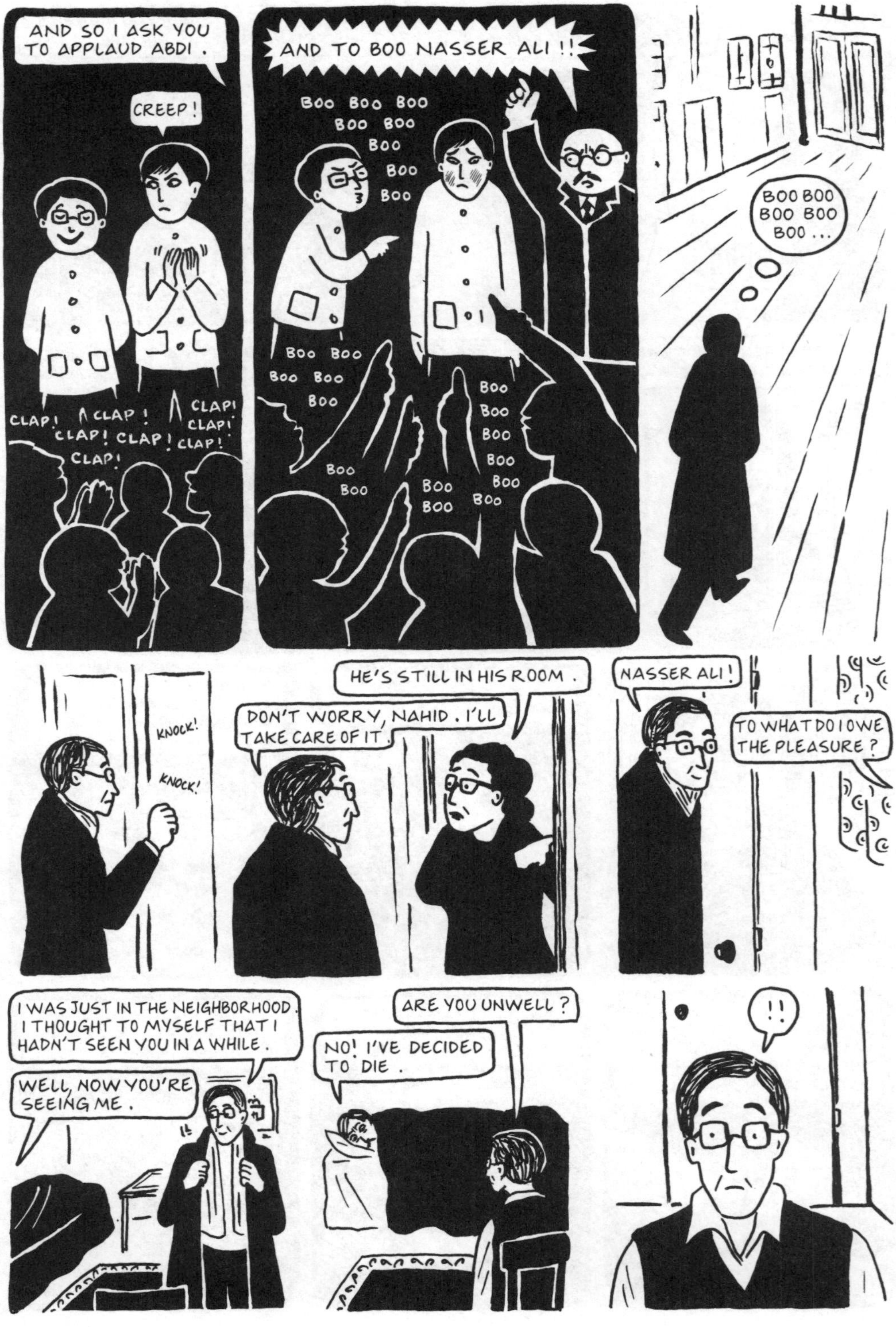
AND SO I ASK YOU TO APPLAUD ABDI.
CREEP!
CLAP! CLAP! CLAP! CLAP! CLAP! CLAP! CLAP! CLAP!
AND TO BOO NASSER ALI!!
BOO BOO BOO BOO BOO BOO BOO BOO
BOO BOO BOO BOO BOO
BOO BOO BOO BOO BOO BOO BOO BOO BOO BOO BOO
BOO BOO BOO BOO BOO...
KNOCK! KNOCK!
HE'S STILL IN HIS ROOM.
DON'T WORRY, NAHID. I'LL TAKE CARE OF IT.
NASSER ALI!
TO WHAT DO I OWE THE PLEASURE?
I WAS JUST IN THE NEIGHBORHOOD. I THOUGHT TO MYSELF THAT I HADN'T SEEN YOU IN A WHILE.
WELL, NOW YOU'RE SEEING ME.
ARE YOU UNWELL?
NO! I'VE DECIDED TO DIE.
!!

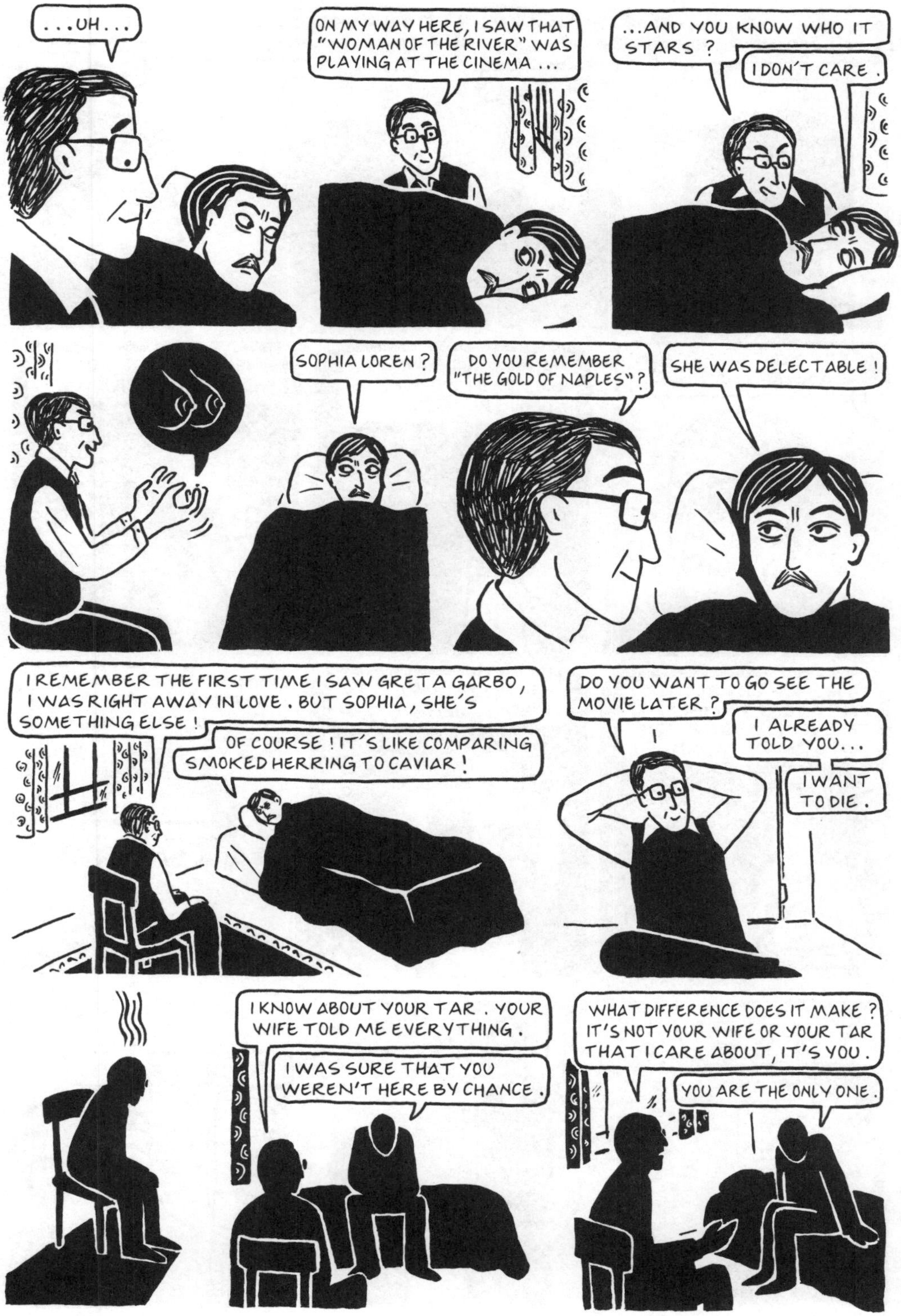
...UH...
ON MY WAY HERE, I SAW THAT "WOMAN OF THE RIVER" WAS PLAYING AT THE CINEMA ...
...AND YOU KNOW WHO IT STARS ?
I DON'T CARE .
SOPHIA LOREN ?
DO YOU REMEMBER "THE GOLD OF NAPLES" ?
SHE WAS DELECTABLE !
I REMEMBER THE FIRST TIME I SAW GRETA GARBO, I WAS RIGHT AWAY IN LOVE . BUT SOPHIA, SHE'S SOMETHING ELSE !
OF COURSE ! IT'S LIKE COMPARING SMOKED HERRING TO CAVIAR !
DO YOU WANT TO GO SEE THE MOVIE LATER ?
I ALREADY TOLD YOU...
I WANT TO DIE .
I KNOW ABOUT YOUR TAR . YOUR WIFE TOLD ME EVERYTHING .
I WAS SURE THAT YOU WEREN'T HERE BY CHANCE .
WHAT DIFFERENCE DOES IT MAKE ? IT'S NOT YOUR WIFE OR YOUR TAR THAT I CARE ABOUT, IT'S YOU .
YOU ARE THE ONLY ONE .

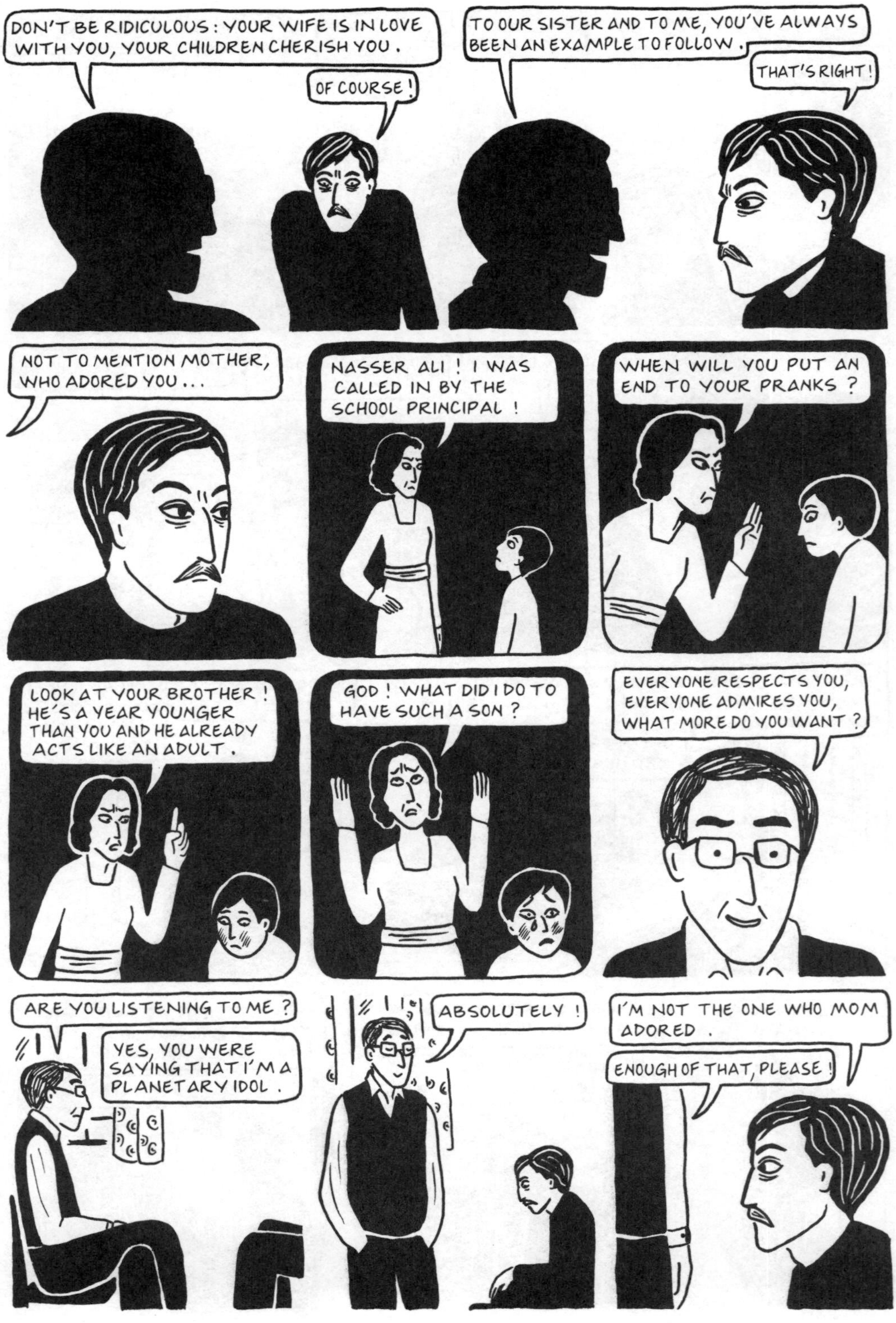
DON'T BE RIDICULOUS : YOUR WIFE IS IN LOVE WITH YOU, YOUR CHILDREN CHERISH YOU .
OF COURSE !
TO OUR SISTER AND TO ME, YOU'VE ALWAYS BEEN AN EXAMPLE TO FOLLOW .
THAT'S RIGHT !
NOT TO MENTION MOTHER, WHO ADORED YOU . . .
NASSER ALI ! I WAS CALLED IN BY THE SCHOOL PRINCIPAL !
WHEN WILL YOU PUT AN END TO YOUR PRANKS ?
LOOK AT YOUR BROTHER ! HE'S A YEAR YOUNGER THAN YOU AND HE ALREADY ACTS LIKE AN ADULT .
GOD ! WHAT DID I DO TO HAVE SUCH A SON ?
EVERYONE RESPECTS YOU, EVERYONE ADMIRES YOU, WHAT MORE DO YOU WANT ?
ARE YOU LISTENING TO ME ?
YES, YOU WERE SAYING THAT I'M A PLANETARY IDOL .
ABSOLUTELY !
I'M NOT THE ONE WHO MOM ADORED .
ENOUGH OF THAT, PLEASE !

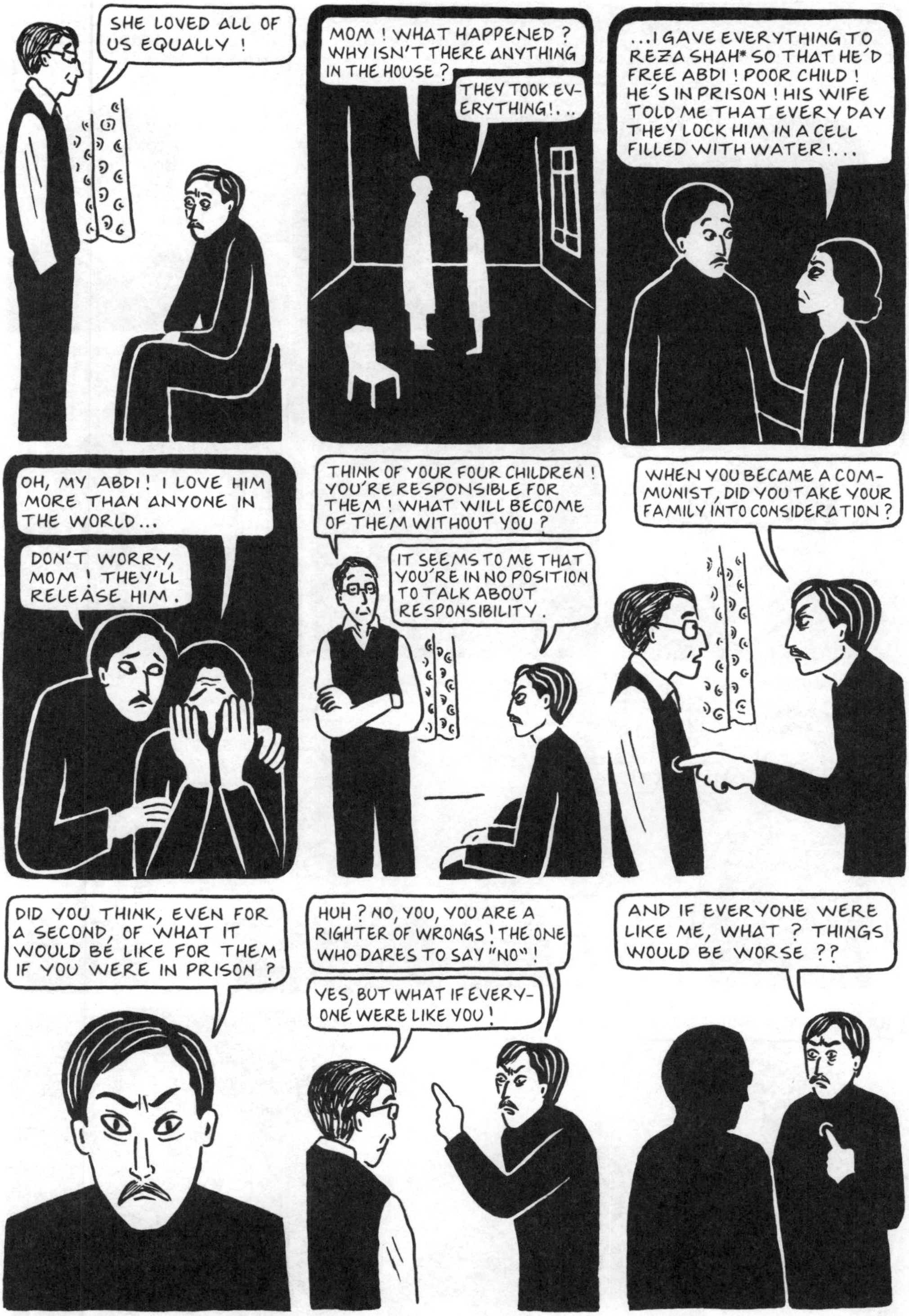
SHE LOVED ALL OF US EQUALLY !
MOM ! WHAT HAPPENED ? WHY ISN'T THERE ANYTHING IN THE HOUSE ?
THEY TOOK EVERYTHING!...
...I GAVE EVERYTHING TO REZA SHAH* SO THAT HE'D FREE ABDI ! POOR CHILD ! HE'S IN PRISON ! HIS WIFE TOLD ME THAT EVERY DAY THEY LOCK HIM IN A CELL FILLED WITH WATER!...
OH, MY ABDI ! I LOVE HIM MORE THAN ANYONE IN THE WORLD...
DON'T WORRY, MOM ! THEY'LL RELEASE HIM.
THINK OF YOUR FOUR CHILDREN ! YOU'RE RESPONSIBLE FOR THEM ! WHAT WILL BECOME OF THEM WITHOUT YOU ?
IT SEEMS TO ME THAT YOU'RE IN NO POSITION TO TALK ABOUT RESPONSIBILITY.
WHEN YOU BECAME A COMMUNIST, DID YOU TAKE YOUR FAMILY INTO CONSIDERATION ?
DID YOU THINK, EVEN FOR A SECOND, OF WHAT IT WOULD BE LIKE FOR THEM IF YOU WERE IN PRISON ?
HUH ? NO, YOU, YOU ARE A RIGHTER OF WRONGS ! THE ONE WHO DARES TO SAY "NO" !
YES, BUT WHAT IF EVERYONE WERE LIKE YOU !
AND IF EVERYONE WERE LIKE ME, WHAT ? THINGS WOULD BE WORSE ??

*THE SHAH OF IRAN'S FATHER.

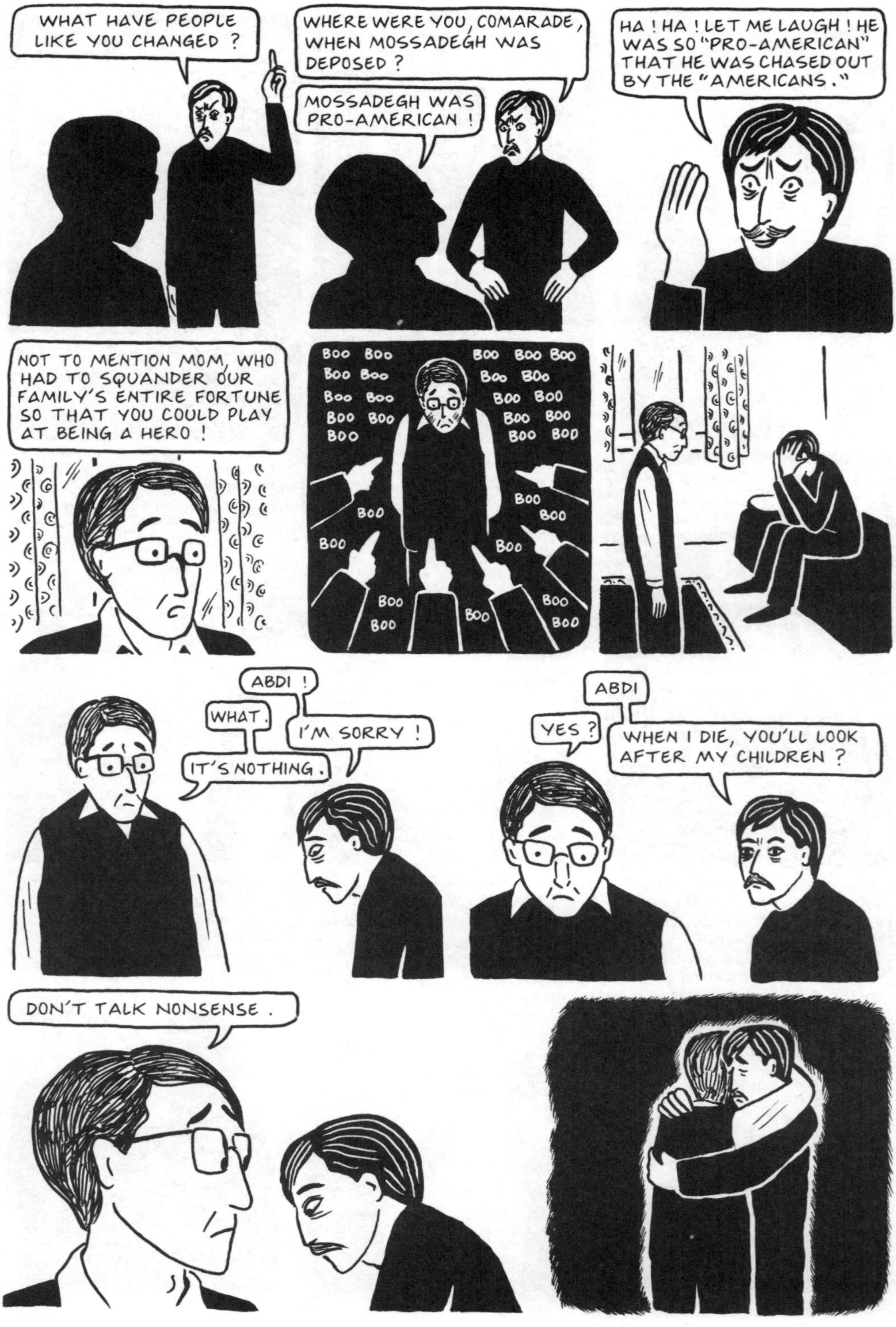
WHAT HAVE PEOPLE LIKE YOU CHANGED ?
WHERE WERE YOU, COMARADE, WHEN MOSSADEGH WAS DEPOSED ?
MOSSADEGH WAS PRO-AMERICAN !
HA ! HA ! LET ME LAUGH ! HE WAS SO "PRO-AMERICAN" THAT HE WAS CHASED OUT BY THE "AMERICANS."
NOT TO MENTION MOM, WHO HAD TO SQUANDER OUR FAMILY'S ENTIRE FORTUNE SO THAT YOU COULD PLAY AT BEING A HERO !
BOO BOO BOO BOO BOO BOO BOO BOO BOO BOO BOO BOO BOO BOO BOO BOO BOO BOO BOO BOO BOO BOO BOO BOO BOO BOO BOO BOO BOO BOO BOO
ABDI !
WHAT.
I'M SORRY !
IT'S NOTHING.
ABDI
YES ?
WHEN I DIE, YOU'LL LOOK AFTER MY CHILDREN ?
DON'T TALK NONSENSE .

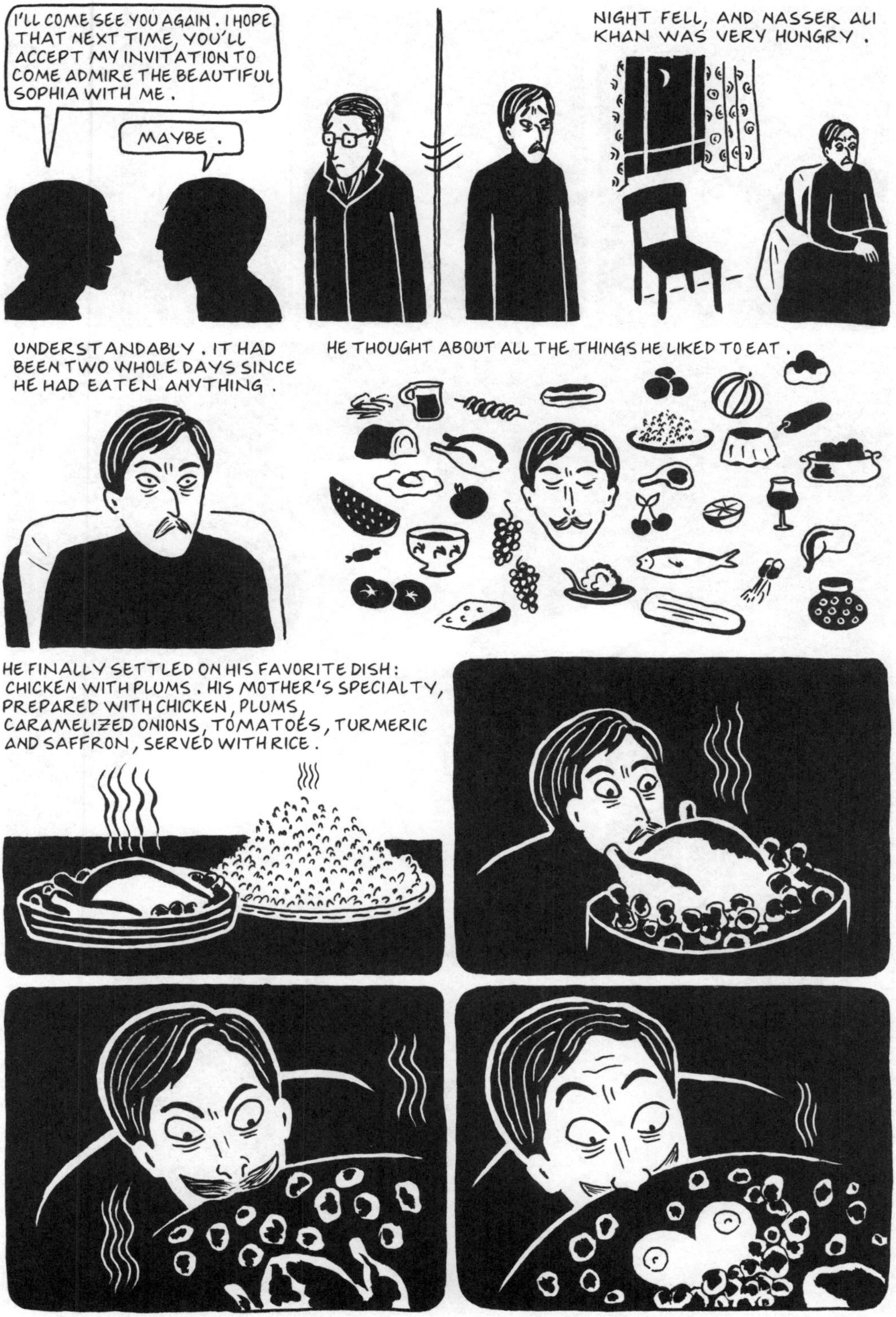

I'LL COME SEE YOU AGAIN. I HOPE THAT NEXT TIME, YOU'LL ACCEPT MY INVITATION TO COME ADMIRE THE BEAUTIFUL SOPHIA WITH ME.
MAYBE.
NIGHT FELL, AND NASSER ALI KHAN WAS VERY HUNGRY.
UNDERSTANDABLY. IT HAD BEEN TWO WHOLE DAYS SINCE HE HAD EATEN ANYTHING.
HE THOUGHT ABOUT ALL THE THINGS HE LIKED TO EAT.
HE FINALLY SETTLED ON HIS FAVORITE DISH: CHICKEN WITH PLUMS. HIS MOTHER'S SPECIALTY, PREPARED WITH CHICKEN, PLUMS, CARAMELIZED ONIONS, TOMATOES, TURMERIC AND SAFFRON, SERVED WITH RICE.

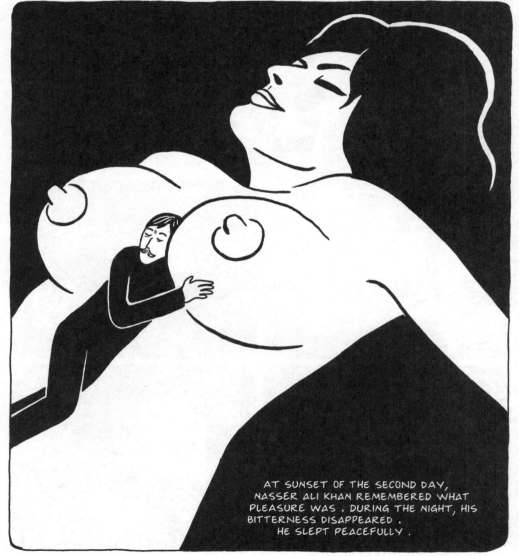

AT SUNSET OF THE SECOND DAY, NASSER ALI KHAN REMEMBERED WHAT PLEASURE WAS . DURING THE NIGHT, HIS BITTERNESS DISAPPEARED . HE SLEPT PEACEFULLY .

THE THIRD DAY

NOVEMBER 17, 1958

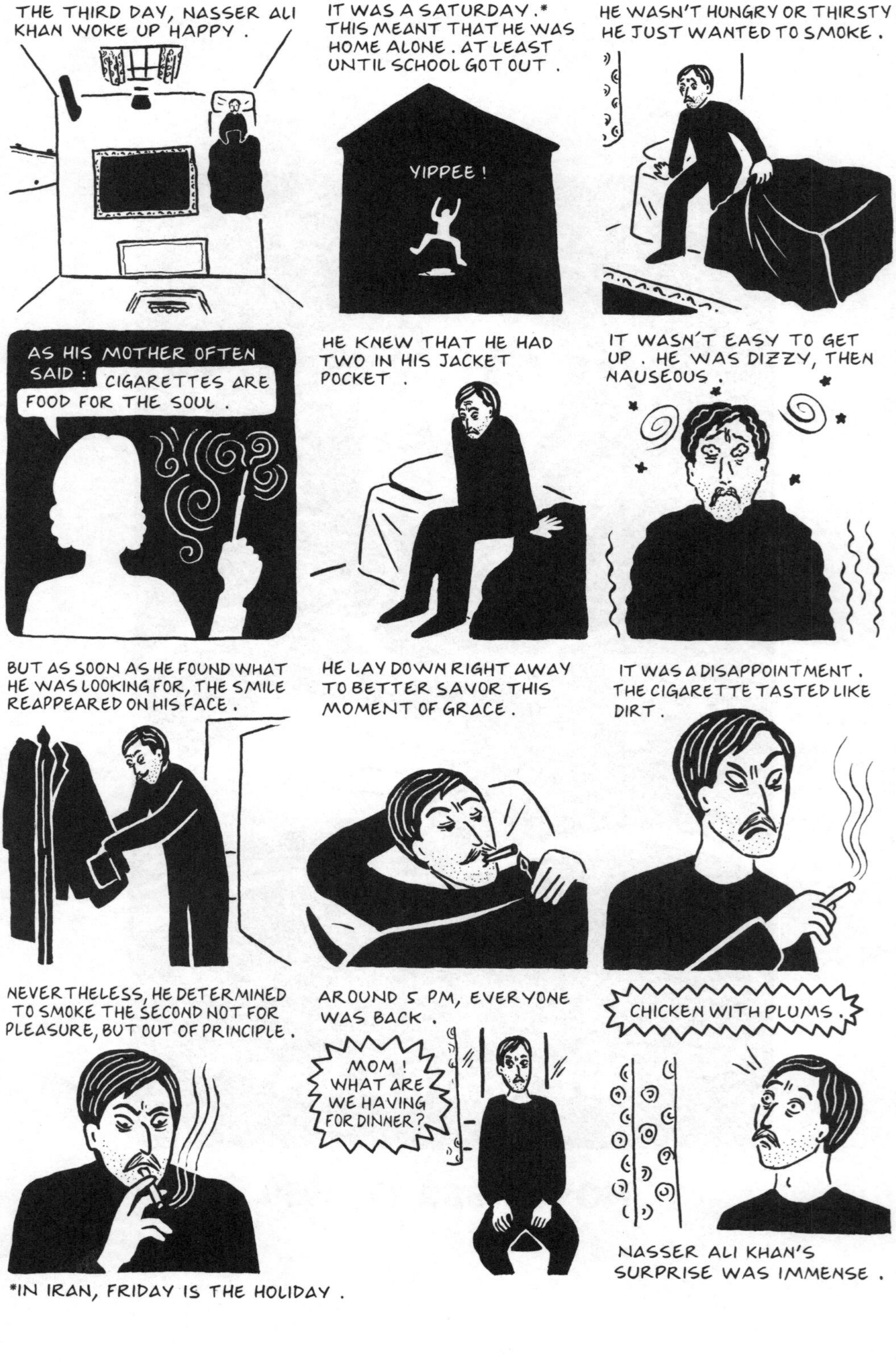
THE THIRD DAY, NASSER ALI KHAN WOKE UP HAPPY.
IT WAS A SATURDAY.* THIS MEANT THAT HE WAS HOME ALONE. AT LEAST UNTIL SCHOOL GOT OUT.
YIPPEE!
HE WASN'T HUNGRY OR THIRSTY. HE JUST WANTED TO SMOKE.
AS HIS MOTHER OFTEN SAID:
CIGARETTES ARE FOOD FOR THE SOUL.
HE KNEW THAT HE HAD TWO IN HIS JACKET POCKET.
IT WASN'T EASY TO GET UP. HE WAS DIZZY, THEN NAUSEOUS.
BUT AS SOON AS HE FOUND WHAT HE WAS LOOKING FOR, THE SMILE REAPPEARED ON HIS FACE.
HE LAY DOWN RIGHT AWAY TO BETTER SAVOR THIS MOMENT OF GRACE.
IT WAS A DISAPPOINTMENT. THE CIGARETTE TASTED LIKE DIRT.
NEVERTHELESS, HE DETERMINED TO SMOKE THE SECOND NOT FOR PLEASURE, BUT OUT OF PRINCIPLE.
AROUND 5 PM, EVERYONE WAS BACK.
MOM! WHAT ARE WE HAVING FOR DINNER?
CHICKEN WITH PLUMS.
NASSER ALI KHAN'S SURPRISE WAS IMMENSE.
*IN IRAN, FRIDAY IS THE HOLIDAY.

FINALLY, THAT NIGHT, HOPING FOR A POSSIBLE RECONCILIATION, NAHID DECIDED TO SERVE A PLATE TO HER HUSBAND.

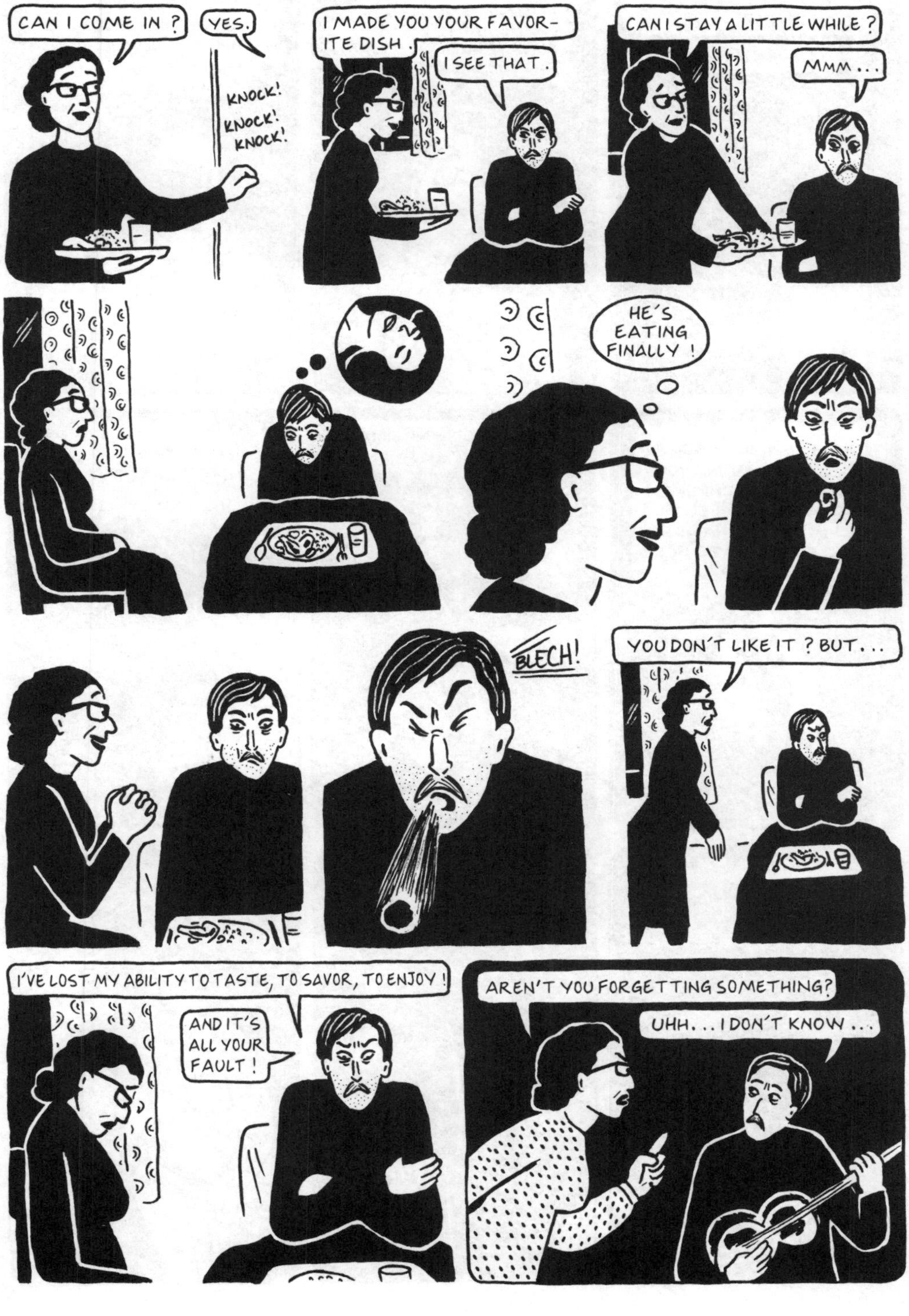

CAN I COME IN?
YES.
KNOCK! KNOCK! KNOCK!
I MADE YOU YOUR FAVORITE DISH.
I SEE THAT.
CAN I STAY A LITTLE WHILE?
MMM...
HE'S EATING FINALLY!
BLECH!
YOU DON'T LIKE IT? BUT...
I'VE LOST MY ABILITY TO TASTE, TO SAVOR, TO ENJOY!
AND IT'S ALL YOUR FAULT!
AREN'T YOU FORGETTING SOMETHING?
UHH... I DON'T KNOW...

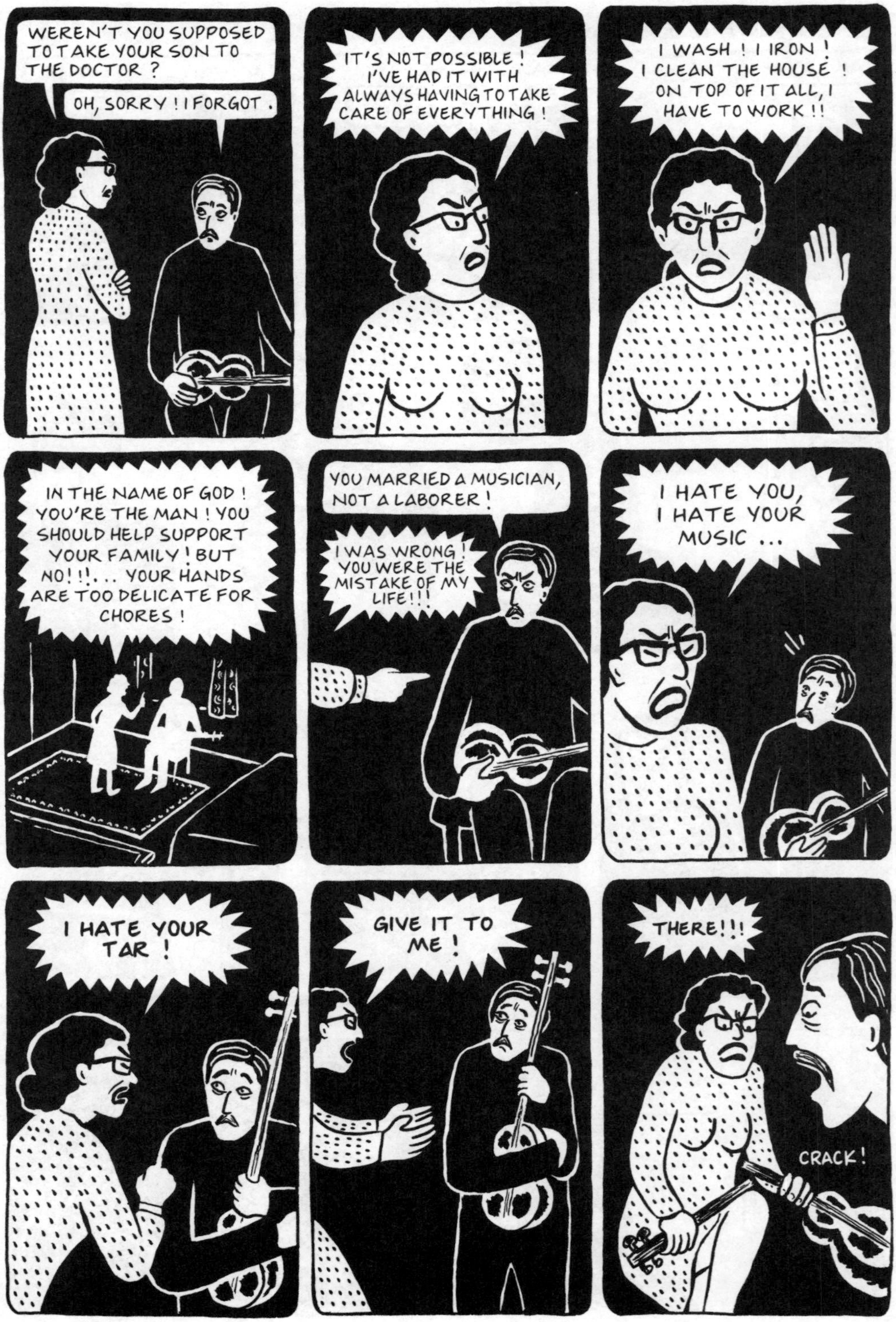

WEREN'T YOU SUPPOSED TO TAKE YOUR SON TO THE DOCTOR ?
OH, SORRY ! I FORGOT .
IT'S NOT POSSIBLE ! I'VE HAD IT WITH ALWAYS HAVING TO TAKE CARE OF EVERYTHING !
I WASH ! I IRON ! I CLEAN THE HOUSE ! ON TOP OF IT ALL, I HAVE TO WORK !!
IN THE NAME OF GOD ! YOU'RE THE MAN ! YOU SHOULD HELP SUPPORT YOUR FAMILY ! BUT NO! !!. . . YOUR HANDS ARE TOO DELICATE FOR CHORES !
YOU MARRIED A MUSICIAN, NOT A LABORER !
I WAS WRONG ! YOU WERE THE MISTAKE OF MY LIFE!!!
I HATE YOU, I HATE YOUR MUSIC ...
I HATE YOUR TAR !
GIVE IT TO ME !
THERE!!!
CRACK!

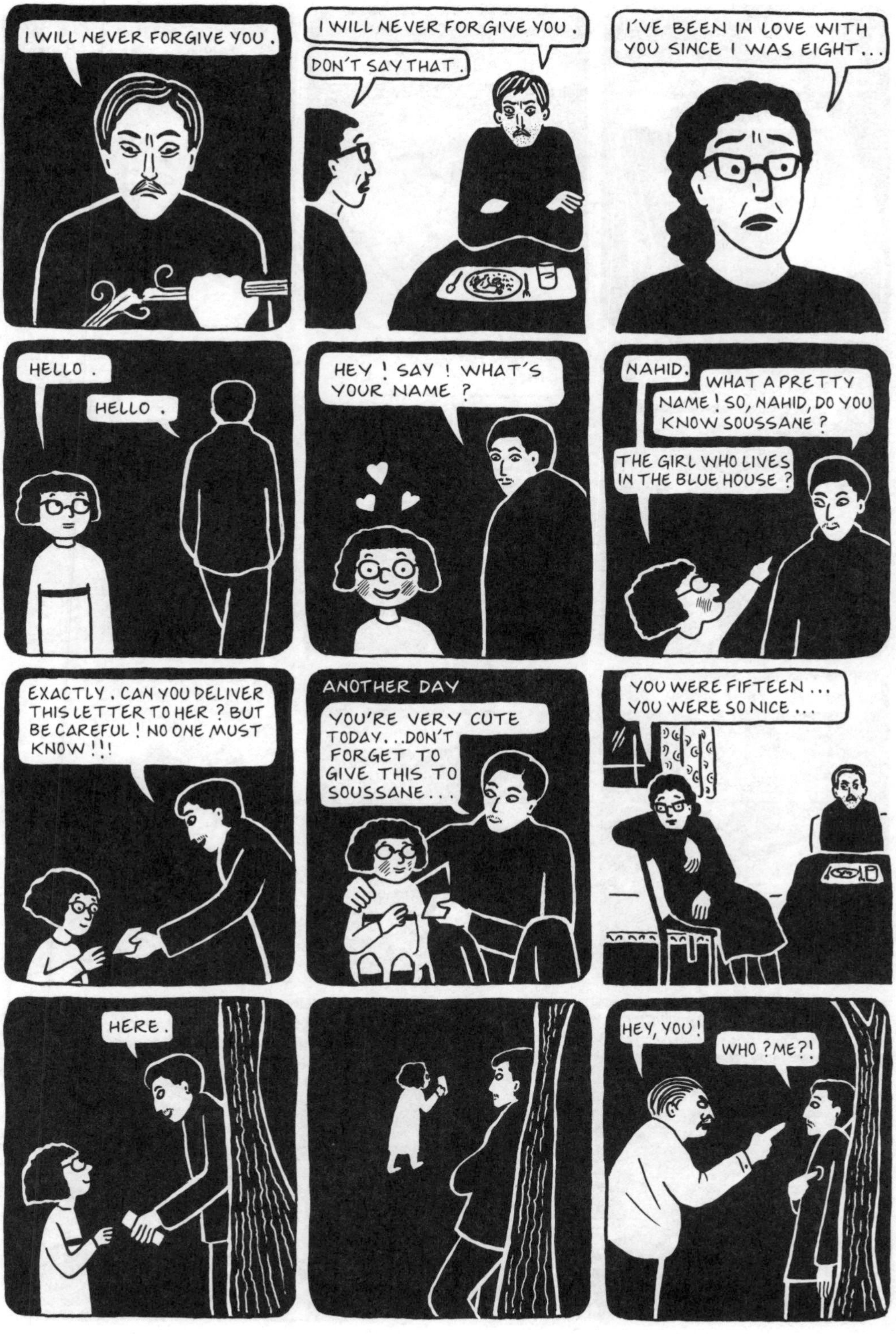
I WILL NEVER FORGIVE YOU.
I WILL NEVER FORGIVE YOU.
DON'T SAY THAT.
I'VE BEEN IN LOVE WITH YOU SINCE I WAS EIGHT...
HELLO.
HELLO.
HEY! SAY! WHAT'S YOUR NAME?
NAHID.
WHAT A PRETTY NAME! SO, NAHID, DO YOU KNOW SOUSSANE?
THE GIRL WHO LIVES IN THE BLUE HOUSE?
EXACTLY. CAN YOU DELIVER THIS LETTER TO HER? BUT BE CAREFUL! NO ONE MUST KNOW!!!
ANOTHER DAY
YOU'RE VERY CUTE TODAY...DON'T FORGET TO GIVE THIS TO SOUSSANE...
YOU WERE FIFTEEN... YOU WERE SO NICE...
HERE.
HEY, YOU!
WHO? ME?!

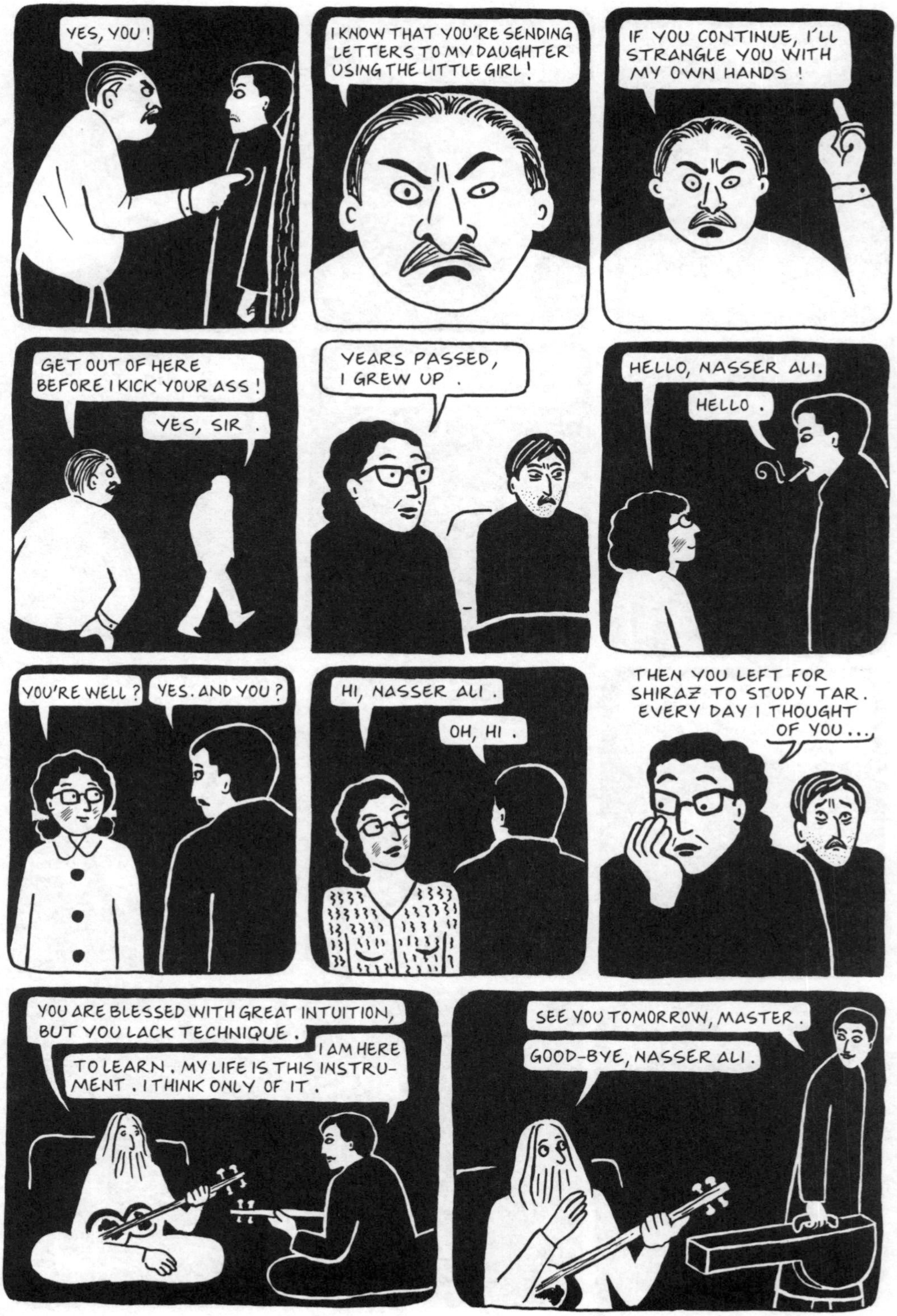
YES, YOU !
I KNOW THAT YOU'RE SENDING LETTERS TO MY DAUGHTER USING THE LITTLE GIRL !
IF YOU CONTINUE, I'LL STRANGLE YOU WITH MY OWN HANDS !
GET OUT OF HERE BEFORE I KICK YOUR ASS !
YES, SIR .
YEARS PASSED, I GREW UP .
HELLO, NASSER ALI.
HELLO .
YOU'RE WELL ?
YES. AND YOU ?
HI, NASSER ALI .
OH, HI .
THEN YOU LEFT FOR SHIRAZ TO STUDY TAR. EVERY DAY I THOUGHT OF YOU...
YOU ARE BLESSED WITH GREAT INTUITION, BUT YOU LACK TECHNIQUE .
I AM HERE TO LEARN . MY LIFE IS THIS INSTRU-MENT . I THINK ONLY OF IT .
SEE YOU TOMORROW, MASTER .
GOOD-BYE, NASSER ALI .

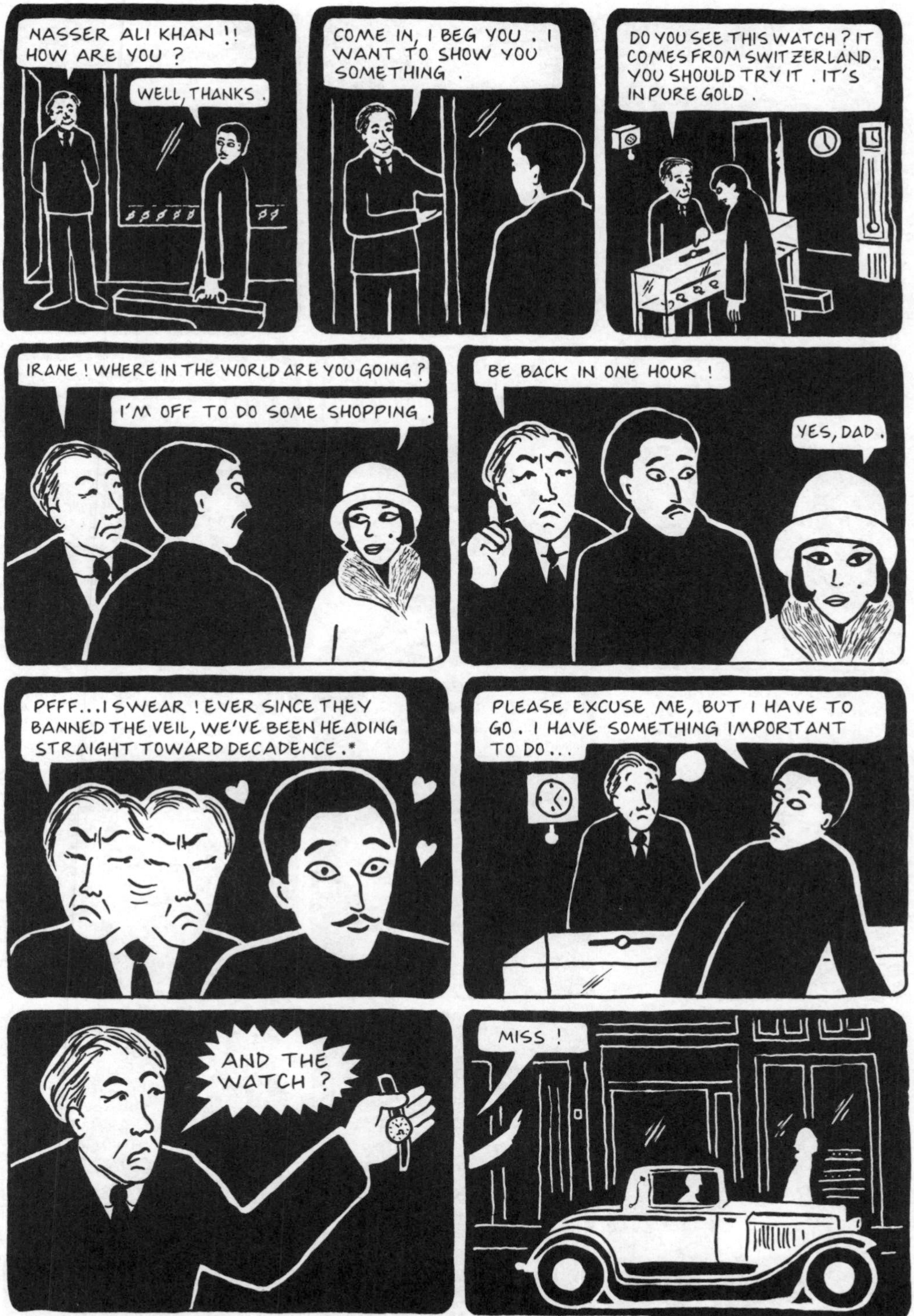
NASSER ALI KHAN !! HOW ARE YOU ?
WELL, THANKS .
COME IN, I BEG YOU . I WANT TO SHOW YOU SOMETHING .
DO YOU SEE THIS WATCH ? IT COMES FROM SWITZERLAND . YOU SHOULD TRY IT . IT'S IN PURE GOLD .
IRANE ! WHERE IN THE WORLD ARE YOU GOING ?
I'M OFF TO DO SOME SHOPPING .
BE BACK IN ONE HOUR !
YES, DAD .
PFFF... I SWEAR ! EVER SINCE THEY BANNED THE VEIL, WE'VE BEEN HEADING STRAIGHT TOWARD DECADENCE .*
PLEASE EXCUSE ME, BUT I HAVE TO GO . I HAVE SOMETHING IMPORTANT TO DO...
AND THE WATCH ?
MISS !

*IN JANUARY 1936, REZA SHAH FORBADE THE WEARING OF THE VEIL IN IRAN .

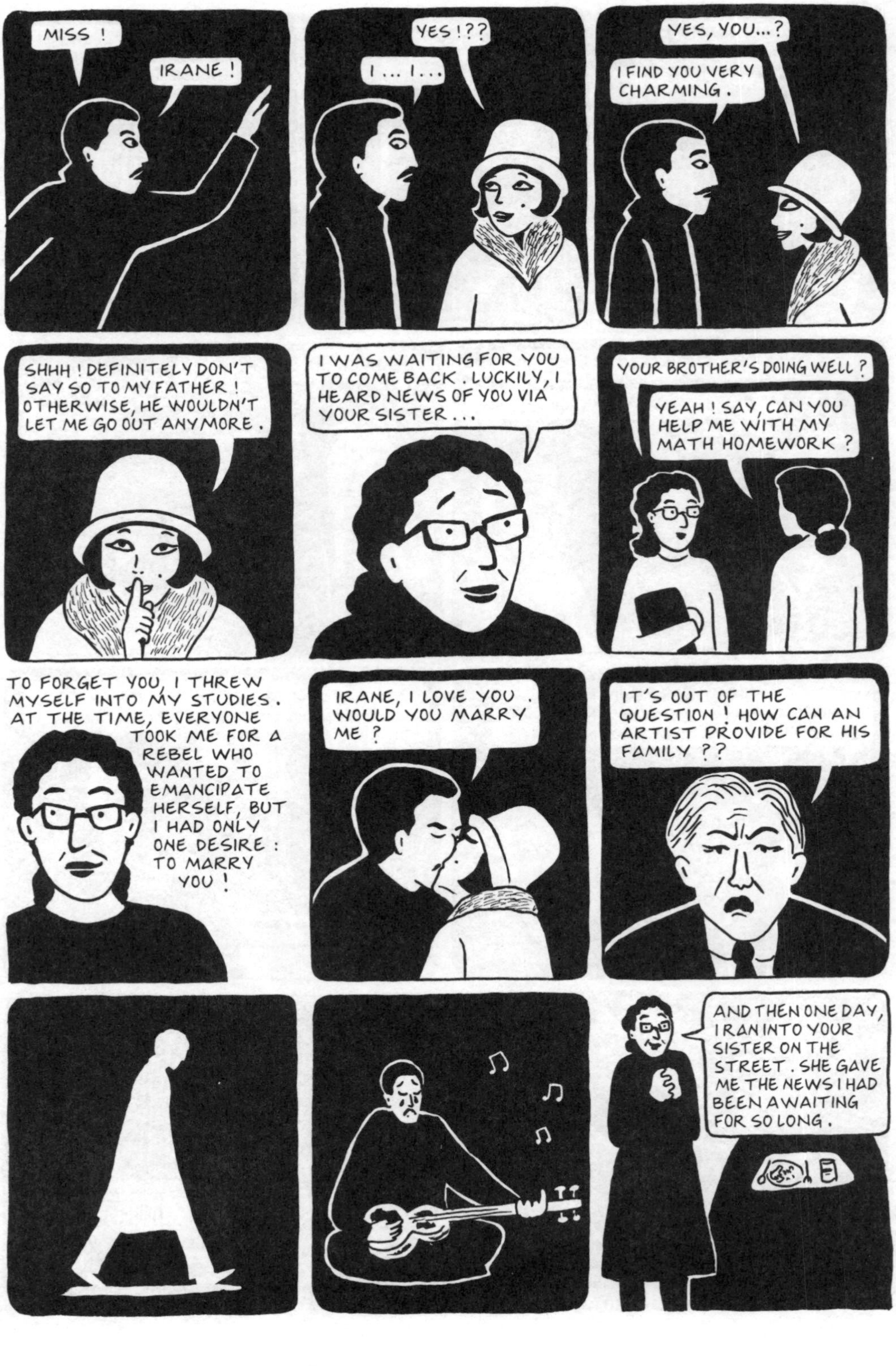
MISS !
IRANE !
YES !??
I ... I ...
YES, YOU...?
I FIND YOU VERY CHARMING.
SHHH ! DEFINITELY DON'T SAY SO TO MY FATHER ! OTHERWISE, HE WOULDN'T LET ME GO OUT ANYMORE.
I WAS WAITING FOR YOU TO COME BACK. LUCKILY, I HEARD NEWS OF YOU VIA YOUR SISTER...
YOUR BROTHER'S DOING WELL ?
YEAH ! SAY, CAN YOU HELP ME WITH MY MATH HOMEWORK ?
TO FORGET YOU, I THREW MYSELF INTO MY STUDIES. AT THE TIME, EVERYONE TOOK ME FOR A REBEL WHO WANTED TO EMANCIPATE HERSELF, BUT I HAD ONLY ONE DESIRE : TO MARRY YOU !
IRANE, I LOVE YOU. WOULD YOU MARRY ME ?
IT'S OUT OF THE QUESTION ! HOW CAN AN ARTIST PROVIDE FOR HIS FAMILY ??
AND THEN ONE DAY, I RAN INTO YOUR SISTER ON THE STREET. SHE GAVE ME THE NEWS I HAD BEEN AWAITING FOR SO LONG.

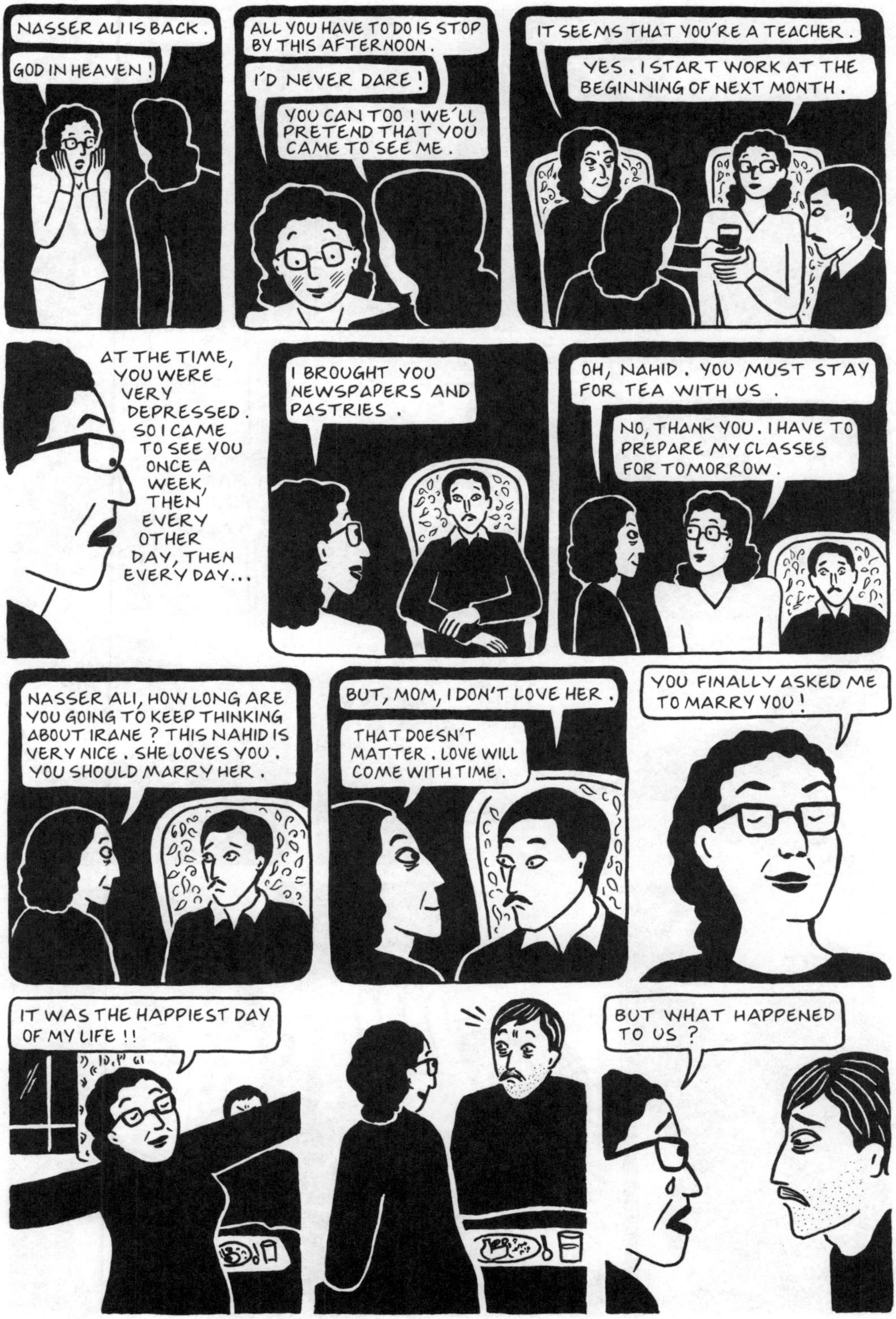
NASSER ALI IS BACK.
GOD IN HEAVEN!
ALL YOU HAVE TO DO IS STOP BY THIS AFTERNOON.
I'D NEVER DARE!
YOU CAN TOO! WE'LL PRETEND THAT YOU CAME TO SEE ME.
IT SEEMS THAT YOU'RE A TEACHER.
YES. I START WORK AT THE BEGINNING OF NEXT MONTH.
AT THE TIME, YOU WERE VERY DEPRESSED. SO I CAME TO SEE YOU ONCE A WEEK, THEN EVERY OTHER DAY, THEN EVERY DAY...
I BROUGHT YOU NEWSPAPERS AND PASTRIES.
OH, NAHID. YOU MUST STAY FOR TEA WITH US.
NO, THANK YOU. I HAVE TO PREPARE MY CLASSES FOR TOMORROW.
NASSER ALI, HOW LONG ARE YOU GOING TO KEEP THINKING ABOUT IRANE? THIS NAHID IS VERY NICE. SHE LOVES YOU. YOU SHOULD MARRY HER.
BUT, MOM, I DON'T LOVE HER.
THAT DOESN'T MATTER. LOVE WILL COME WITH TIME.
YOU FINALLY ASKED ME TO MARRY YOU!
IT WAS THE HAPPIEST DAY OF MY LIFE!!
BUT WHAT HAPPENED TO US?

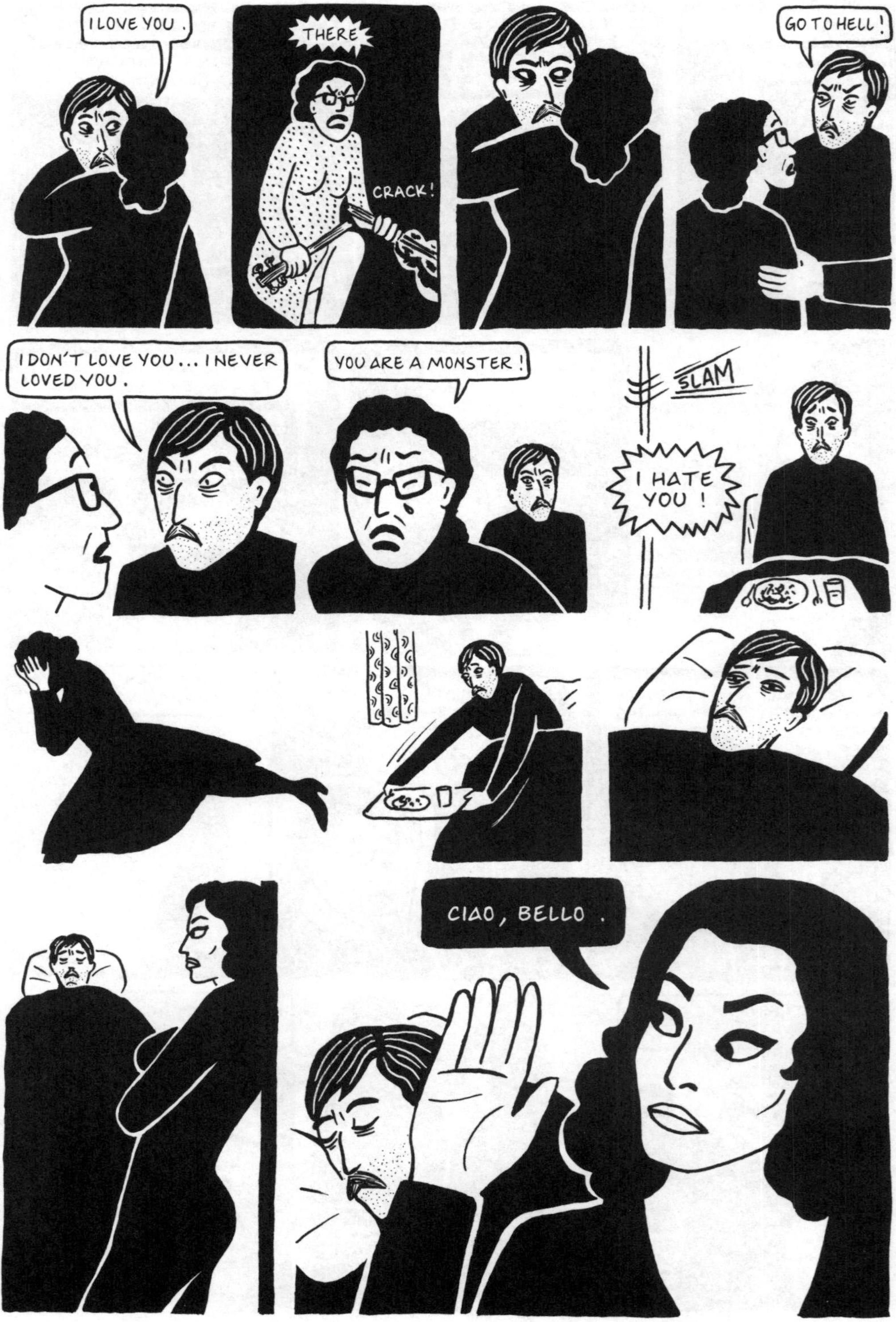
I LOVE YOU.
THERE
CRACK!
GO TO HELL!
I DON'T LOVE YOU... I NEVER LOVED YOU.
YOU ARE A MONSTER!
SLAM
I HATE YOU!
CIAO, BELLO.

THE FOURTH DAY

NOVEMBER 18, 1958

NO DAY IN THE SHORT LIFE OF NASSER ALI KHAN WAS MORE BLEAK THAN NOVEMBER 18, 1958. NOT ONLY HAD HE VICIOUSLY ARGUED WITH HIS WIFE THE DAY BEFORE, BUT TO MAKE MATTERS WORSE, FOR THE FOUR DAYS THAT HE'D BEEN AWAITING DEATH, ONLY HIS YOUNGEST DAUGHTER, FARZANEH, HAD DEVOTED HIM A FEW MINUTES OF HER TIME. THE INGRATITUDE OF HIS THREE OTHER CHILDREN UPSET HIM DEEPLY.

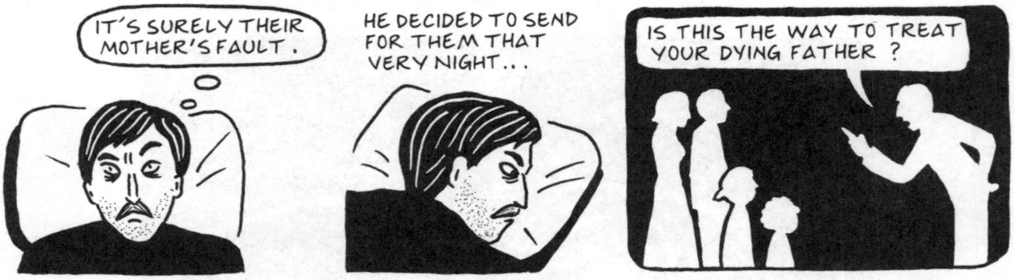
IT'S SURELY THEIR MOTHER'S FAULT.
HE DECIDED TO SEND FOR THEM THAT VERY NIGHT...
IS THIS THE WAY TO TREAT YOUR DYING FATHER ?

BUT WHEN NIGHT CAME, NASSER ALI KHAN CHANGED HIS MIND. CONVINCED THAT HIS END WAS NEAR, HE TOLD HIMSELF THAT HE HAD A DUTY TO LEAVE THEM WITH THE IMAGE OF A GOOD AND GENEROUS MAN. WHICH, AFTER ALL, HE WAS...

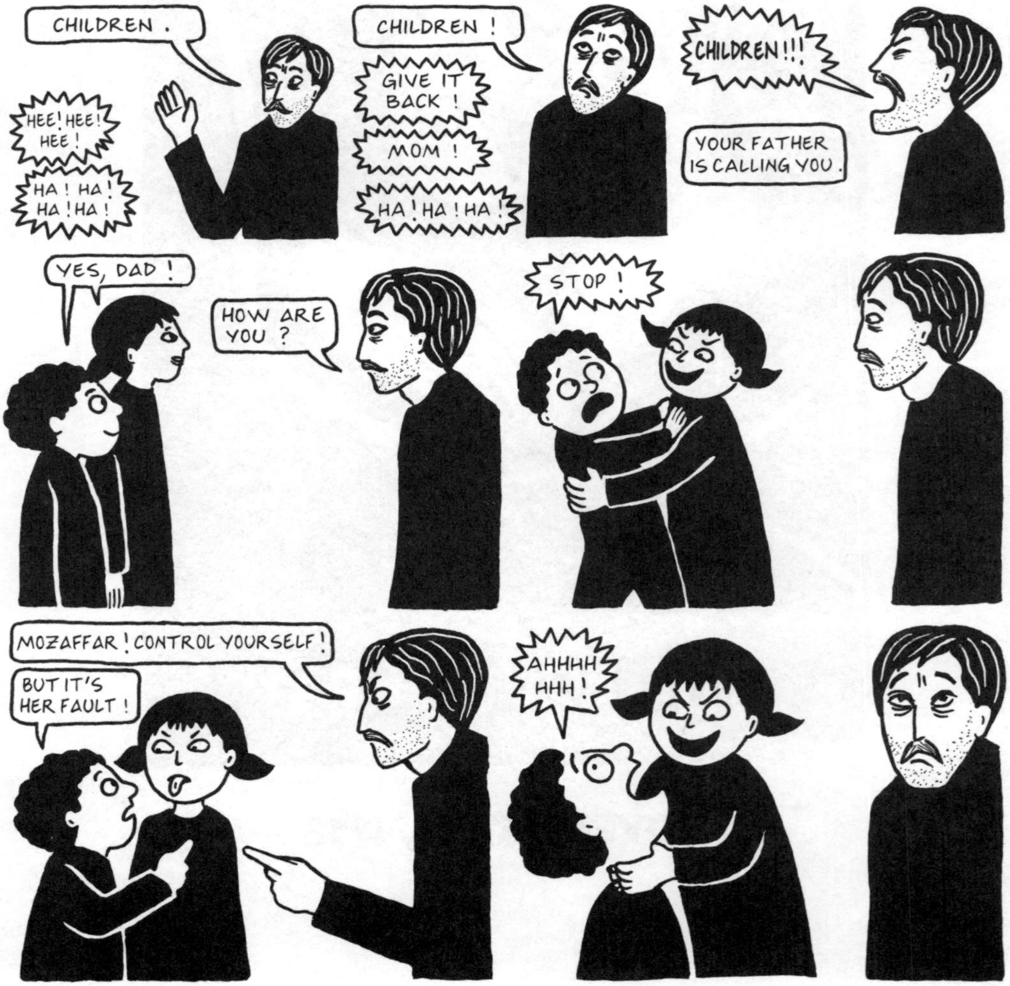
CHILDREN.
HEE! HEE! HEE!
HA! HA! HA! HA!
CHILDREN!
GIVE IT BACK!
MOM!
HA! HA! HA!
CHILDREN!!!
YOUR FATHER IS CALLING YOU.
YES, DAD!
HOW ARE YOU?
STOP!
MOZAFFAR! CONTROL YOURSELF!
BUT IT'S HER FAULT!
AHHHH HHH!

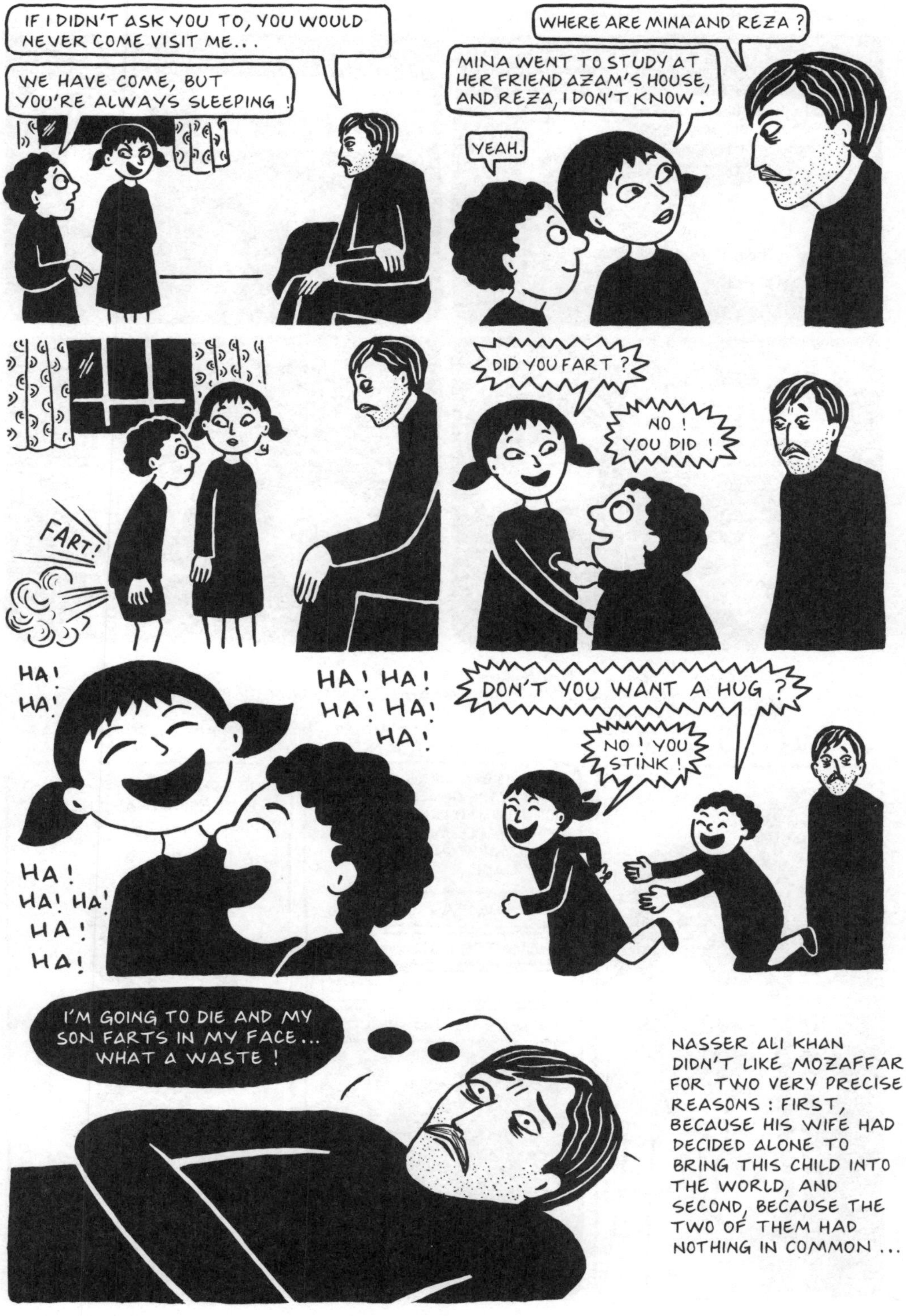
IF I DIDN'T ASK YOU TO, YOU WOULD NEVER COME VISIT ME...
WE HAVE COME, BUT YOU'RE ALWAYS SLEEPING !
WHERE ARE MINA AND REZA ?
MINA WENT TO STUDY AT HER FRIEND AZAM'S HOUSE, AND REZA, I DON'T KNOW.
YEAH.
FART!
DID YOU FART ?
NO ! YOU DID !
HA! HA!
HA! HA! HA! HA! HA!
HA! HA! HA! HA! HA!
DON'T YOU WANT A HUG ?
NO ! YOU STINK !
I'M GOING TO DIE AND MY SON FARTS IN MY FACE... WHAT A WASTE !
NASSER ALI KHAN DIDN'T LIKE MOZAFFAR FOR TWO VERY PRECISE REASONS : FIRST, BECAUSE HIS WIFE HAD DECIDED ALONE TO BRING THIS CHILD INTO THE WORLD, AND SECOND, BECAUSE THE TWO OF THEM HAD NOTHING IN COMMON ...

MOZAFFAR EMBODIED EVERYTHING THAT NASSER ALI KHAN SCORNED :

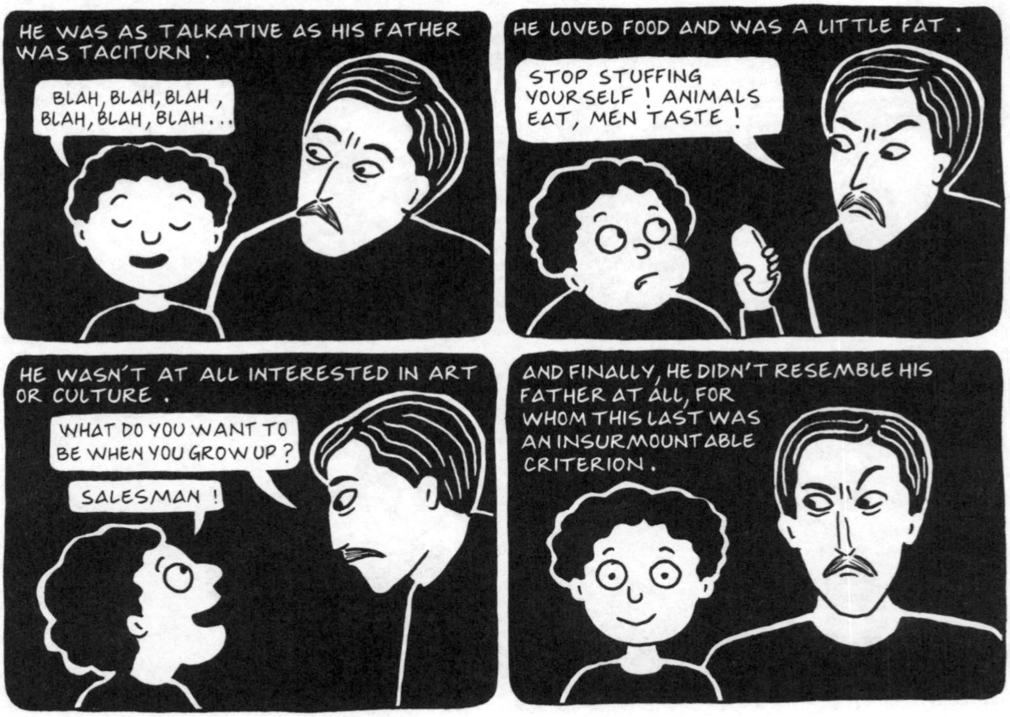
HE WAS AS TALKATIVE AS HIS FATHER WAS TACITURN .
BLAH, BLAH, BLAH, BLAH, BLAH, BLAH...
HE LOVED FOOD AND WAS A LITTLE FAT .
STOP STUFFING YOURSELF ! ANIMALS EAT, MEN TASTE !
HE WASN'T AT ALL INTERESTED IN ART OR CULTURE .
WHAT DO YOU WANT TO BE WHEN YOU GROW UP ?
SALESMAN !
AND FINALLY, HE DIDN'T RESEMBLE HIS FATHER AT ALL, FOR WHOM THIS LAST WAS AN INSURMOUNTABLE CRITERION .

DESTINY PROVED NASSER ALI KHAN RIGHT :
INDEED, MOZAFFAR NEVER BECAME THIN, OR AN ARTIST, OR SUICIDAL, OR EVEN MOROSE AND MELANCHOLIC .
IN 1975, HIS TWENTY-SECOND YEAR, MOZAFFAR MARRIED A CERTAIN GILA WHO WAS STUDYING ECONOMICS AND MANAGEMENT WITH HIM .

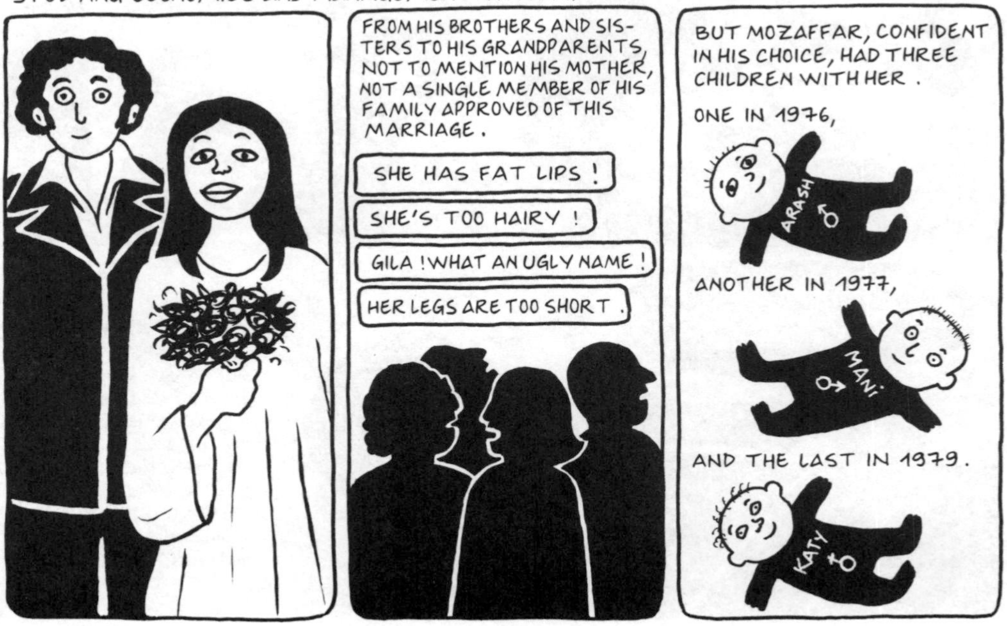
FROM HIS BROTHERS AND SISTERS TO HIS GRANDPARENTS, NOT TO MENTION HIS MOTHER, NOT A SINGLE MEMBER OF HIS FAMILY APPROVED OF THIS MARRIAGE .
SHE HAS FAT LIPS !
SHE'S TOO HAIRY !
GILA ! WHAT AN UGLY NAME !
HER LEGS ARE TOO SHORT .
BUT MOZAFFAR, CONFIDENT IN HIS CHOICE, HAD THREE CHILDREN WITH HER .
ONE IN 1976,
ARASH ♂
ANOTHER IN 1977,
MANI ♂
AND THE LAST IN 1979 .
KATY ♀

ALSO IN 1979, AT THE TIME OF THE IRANIAN REVOLUTION, MOZAFFAR WORKED AS A MANAGER IN THE ARMY AND HIS WIFE WAS AN ACCOUNTANT . EVERYTHING WAS GOING WONDERFULLY . GILA HAD FINALLY BEEN ACCEPTED BY HER IN-LAWS .

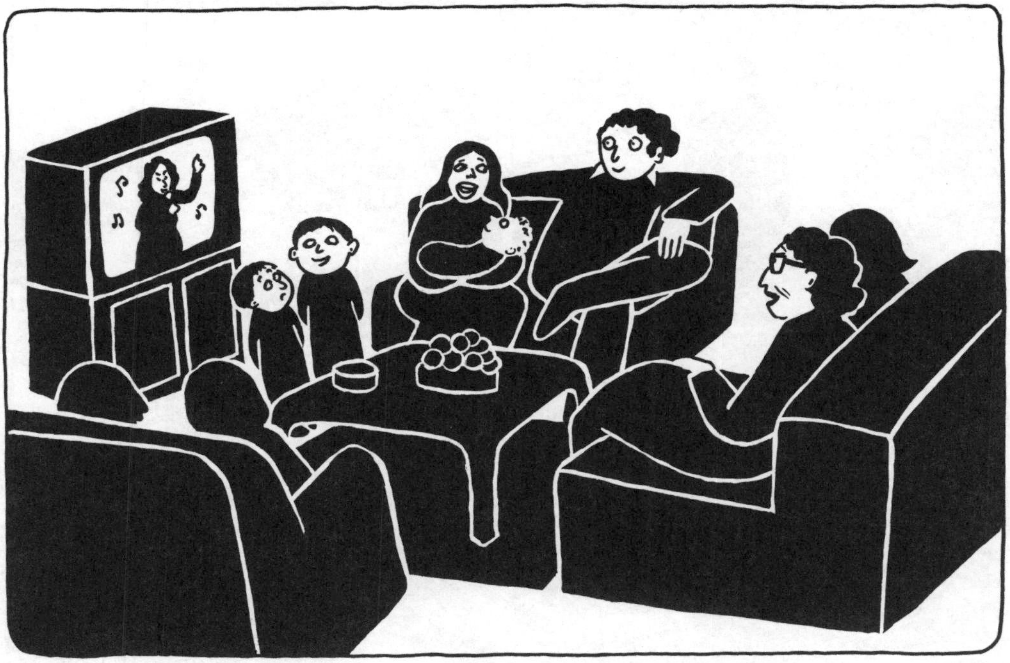

BUT IN 1980 WAR ERUPTED AND THAT WAS THE END OF HAPPINESS .

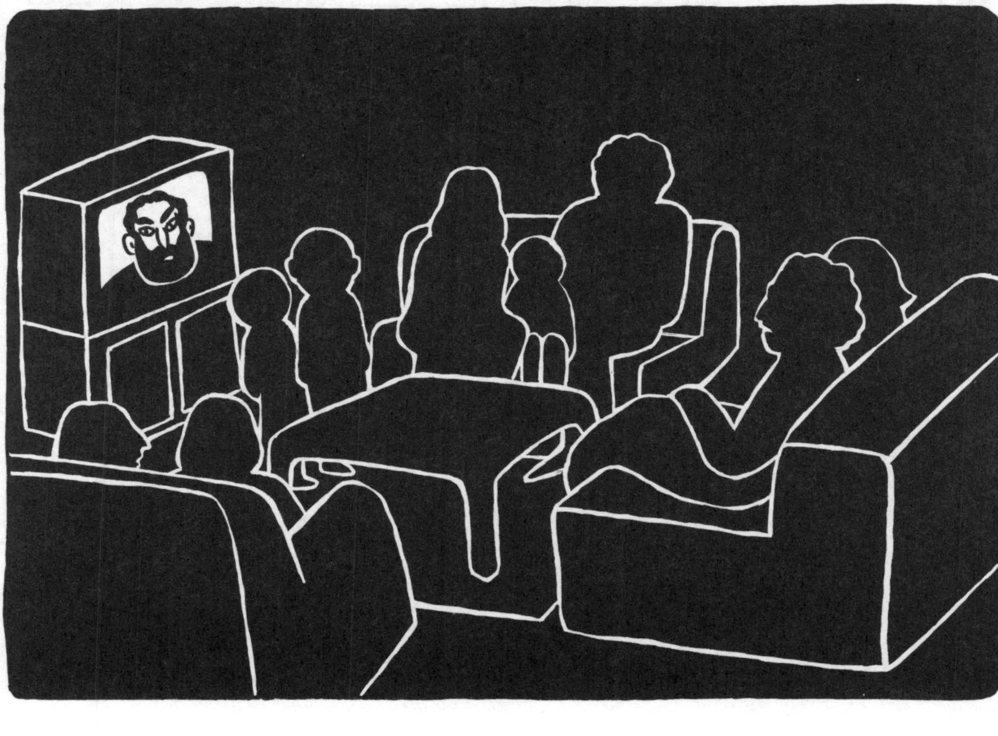

GIVEN THAT MOZAFFAR WORKED FOR THE ARMY, HIS LIFE WAS IN REAL DANGER. ACCOMPANIED BY HIS FAMILY, HE LEFT IRAN AND SETTLED IN THE UNITED STATES.

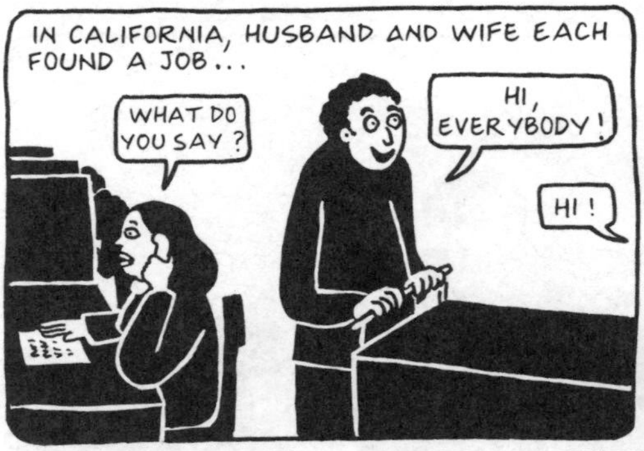
IN CALIFORNIA, HUSBAND AND WIFE EACH FOUND A JOB...
WHAT DO YOU SAY?
HI, EVERYBODY!
HI!

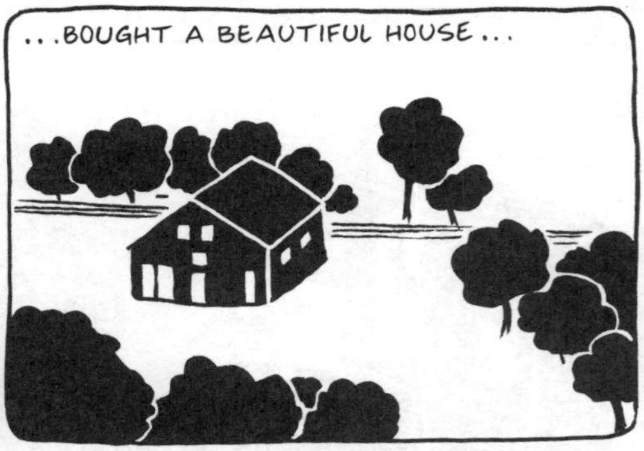
...BOUGHT A BEAUTIFUL HOUSE...

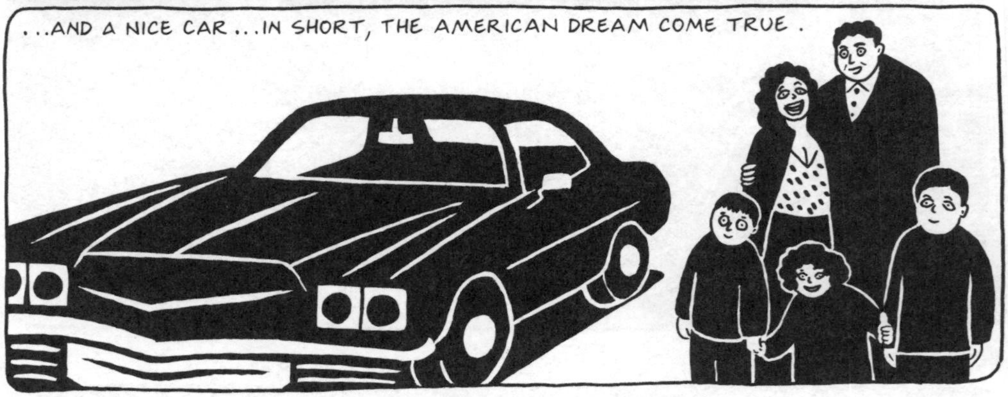
...AND A NICE CAR...IN SHORT, THE AMERICAN DREAM COME TRUE.

EVERYTHING WAS GOING SWIMMINGLY IN THE MOST PERFECT OF WORLDS, EXCEPT...
EXCEPT THAT THEIR CHILDREN HAD SOME SERIOUS WEIGHT PROBLEMS.
MOZAFFAR AND HIS WIFE, ONCE CONSIDERED FAT IN IRAN, LOOKED THIN BESIDE THEM.

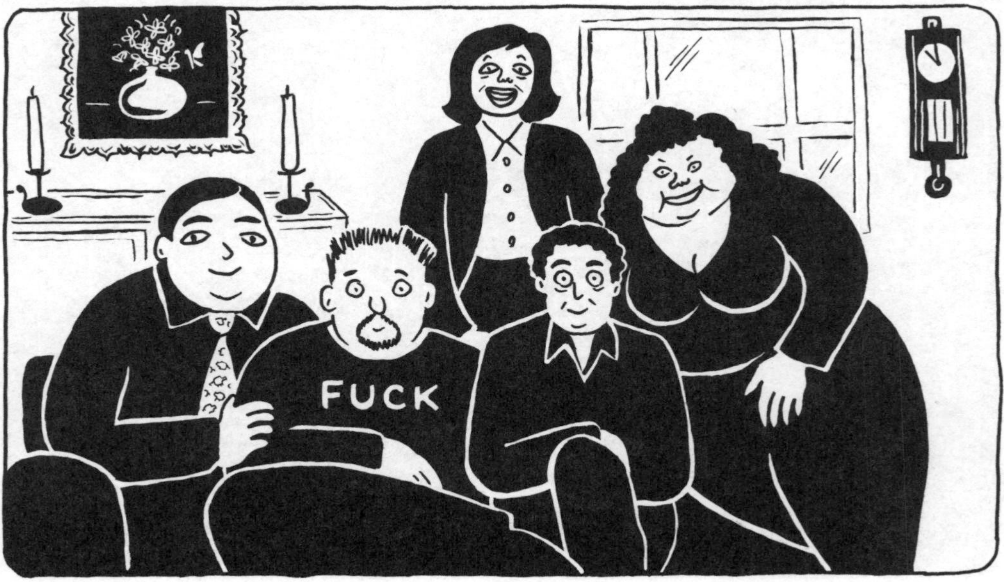
FUCK

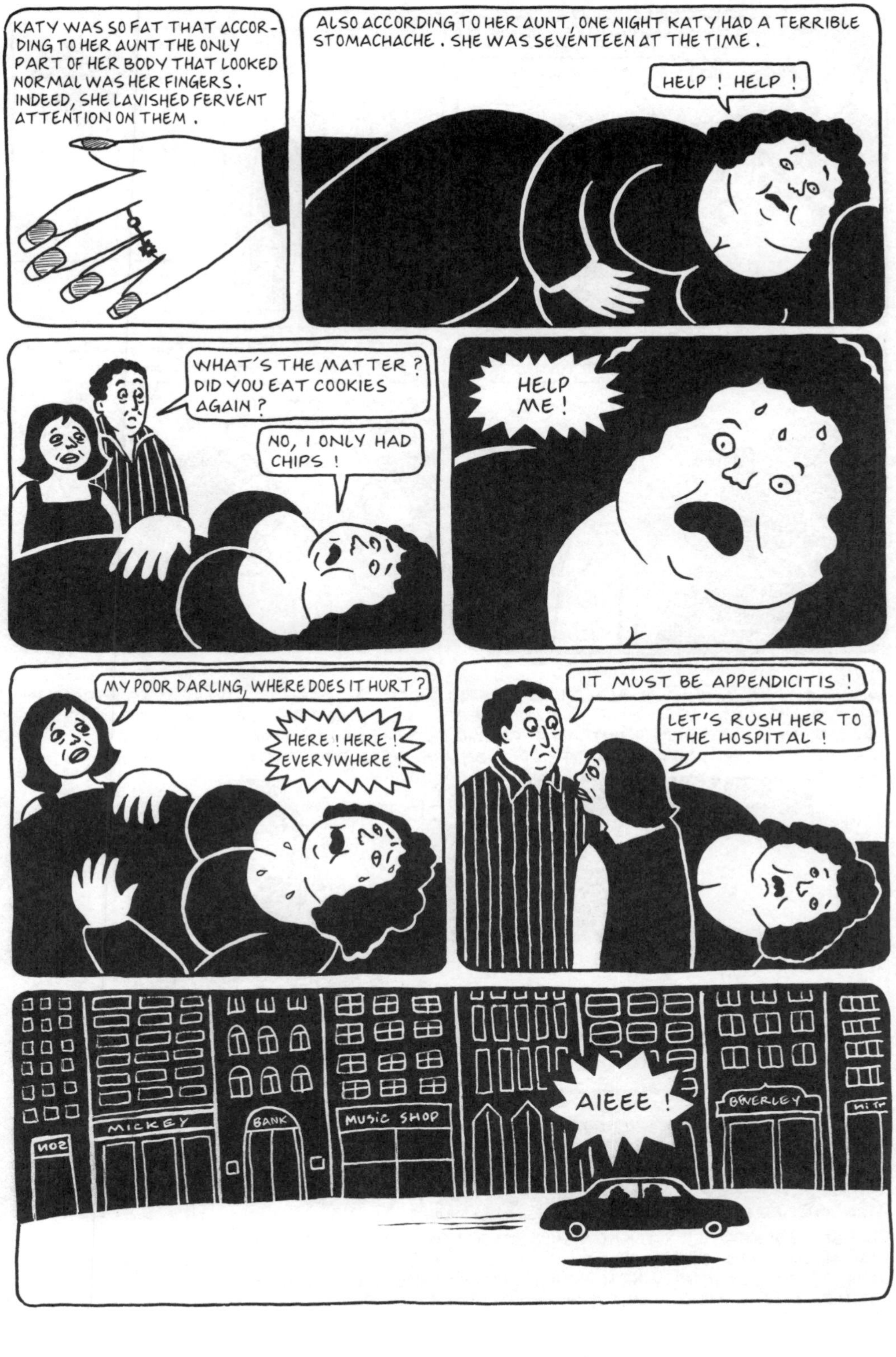
KATY WAS SO FAT THAT ACCORDING TO HER AUNT THE ONLY PART OF HER BODY THAT LOOKED NORMAL WAS HER FINGERS. INDEED, SHE LAVISHED FERVENT ATTENTION ON THEM.
ALSO ACCORDING TO HER AUNT, ONE NIGHT KATY HAD A TERRIBLE STOMACHACHE. SHE WAS SEVENTEEN AT THE TIME.
HELP! HELP!
WHAT'S THE MATTER? DID YOU EAT COOKIES AGAIN?
NO, I ONLY HAD CHIPS!
HELP ME!
MY POOR DARLING, WHERE DOES IT HURT?
HERE! HERE! EVERYWHERE!
IT MUST BE APPENDICITIS!
LET'S RUSH HER TO THE HOSPITAL!
MICKEY
BANK
MUSIC SHOP
AIEEE!
BEVERLEY

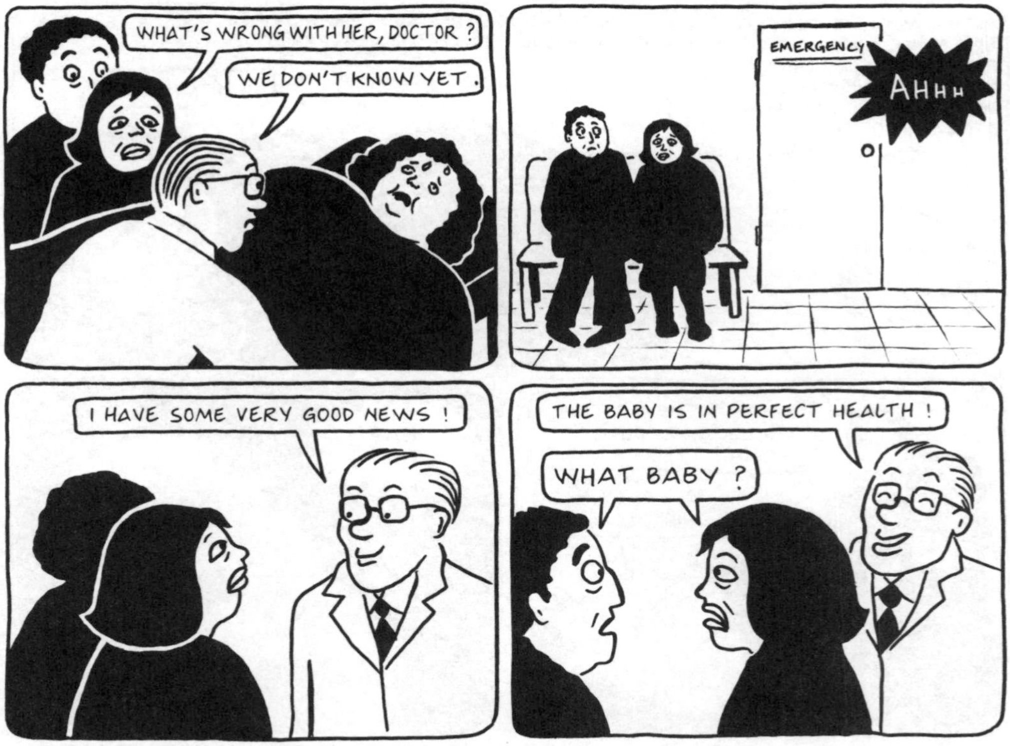
WHAT'S WRONG WITH HER, DOCTOR ?
WE DON'T KNOW YET .
EMERGENCY
AHHH
I HAVE SOME VERY GOOD NEWS !
THE BABY IS IN PERFECT HEALTH !
WHAT BABY ?

APPARENTLY, WHEN THE AUNT IN QUESTION ASKED MOZAFFAR HOW IT WAS POSSIBLE THAT HE WASN'T AWARE OF HIS DAUGHTER'S PREGNANCY, HE ANSWERED THAT IT WAS DIFFICULT TO MAKE OUT AN 8-POUND FETUS IN 400 POUNDS OF MEAT .
THE AUNT ADDED : "I AM SURE THAT EVEN MY NIECE DIDN'T KNOW."

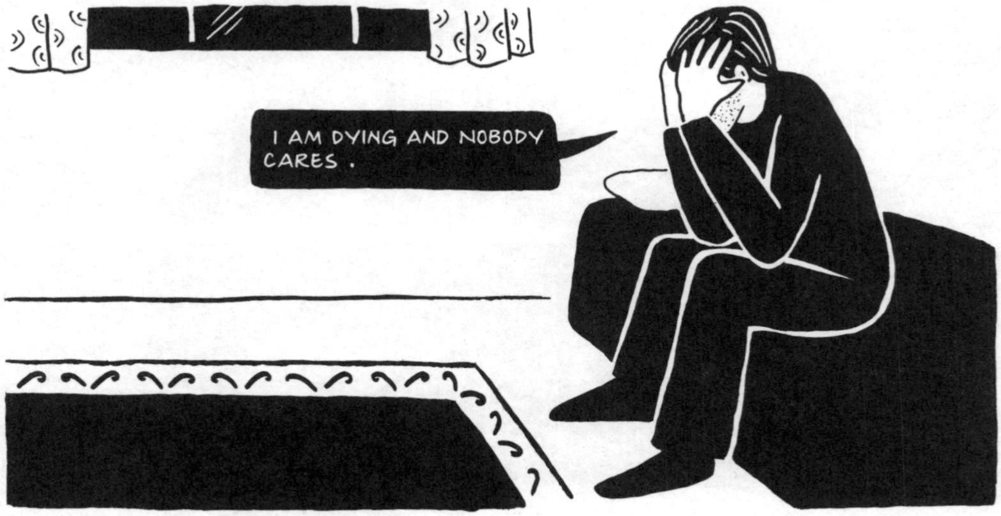
I AM DYING AND NOBODY CARES .

NASSER ALI KHAN DIDN'T KNOW HOW LUCKY HE WAS TO DIE FOUR DAYS LATER . IF HE HAD KNOWN THE STORY OF MOZAFFAR AND HIS DAUGHTER, HE WOULD SURELY HAVE CONTRACTED CANCER, WHICH BY ALL ACCOUNTS IS A MUCH SLOWER AND SIGNIFICANTLY MORE PAINFUL WAY TO DIE .

THE FIFTH DAY

NOVEMBER 19, 1958

AT THE DAWN OF THE FIFTH DAY, NASSER ALI KHAN FELT THAT DEATH COULD NO LONGER BE VERY FAR . HE THOUGHT OF ALL THOSE WHO HAD PASSED AWAY, ALL THOSE WHOM HE HAD LOVED AND WHO WERE GONE, AS THOUGH THEY HAD NEVER EXISTED .
SUDDENLY, HE CAUGHT SIGHT OF HIS MOTHER IN THE CROWD .

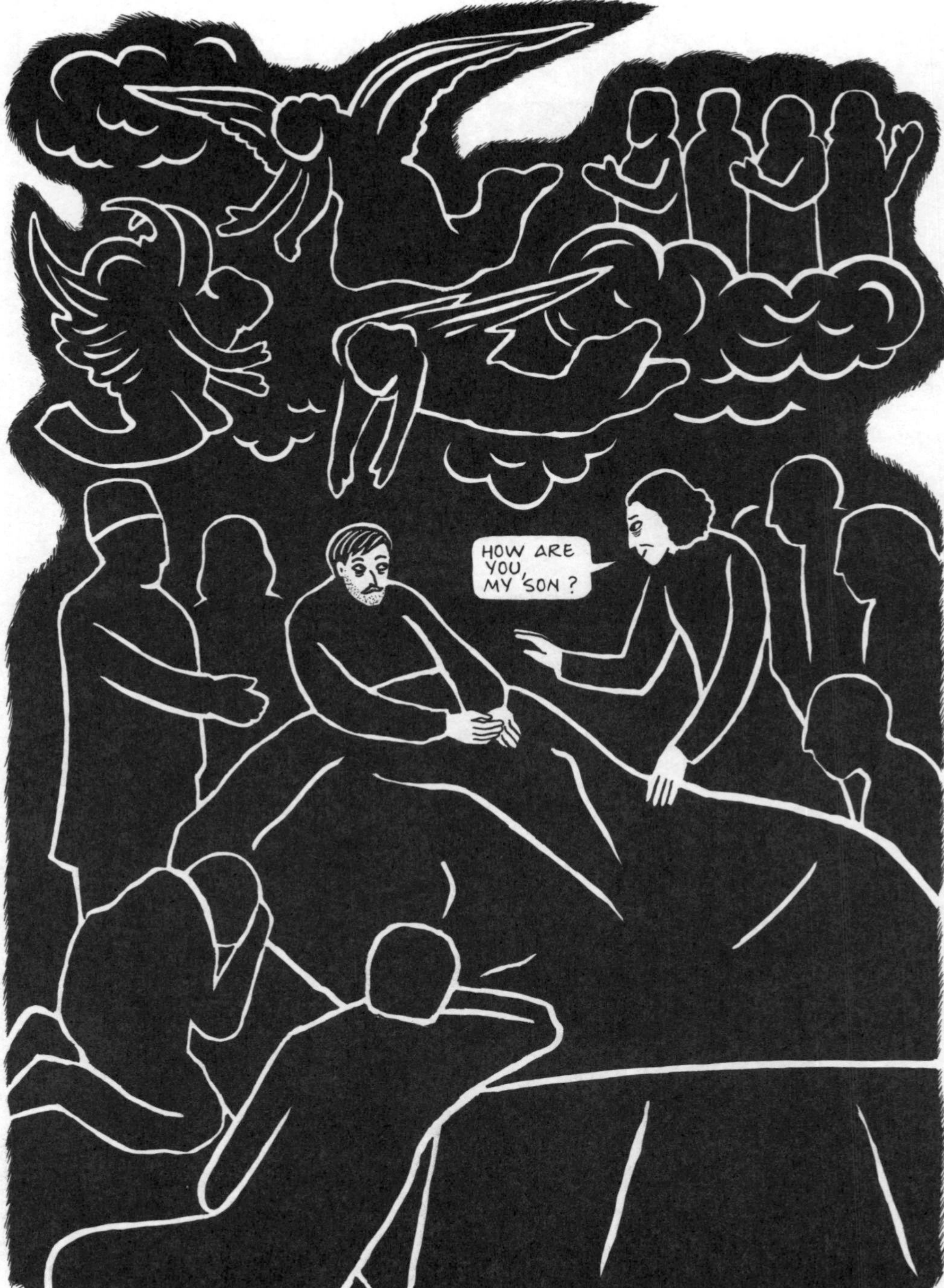
HOW ARE YOU, MY SON ?

LIKE ALL SONS, NASSER ALI KHAN WAS VERY ATTACHED TO HIS MOTHER . HE REMEMBERED THE TIME WHEN SHE FELL GRAVELY ILL, FIFTEEN YEARS BEFORE .

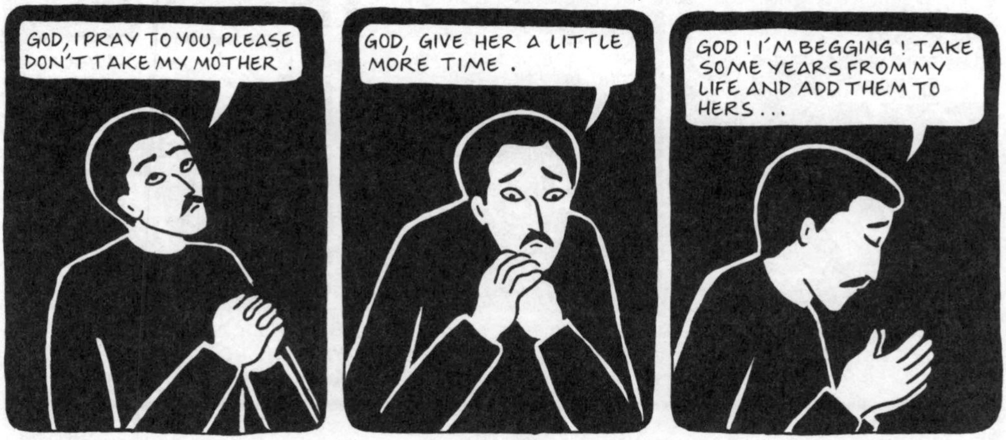
GOD, I PRAY TO YOU, PLEASE DON'T TAKE MY MOTHER .
GOD, GIVE HER A LITTLE MORE TIME .
GOD ! I'M BEGGING ! TAKE SOME YEARS FROM MY LIFE AND ADD THEM TO HERS...

OF COURSE HE NEVER TOLD ANYONE ABOUT HIS NIGHTTIME PRAYERS . THEN ONE DAY HIS MOTHER SUMMONED HIM TO HER ROOM :

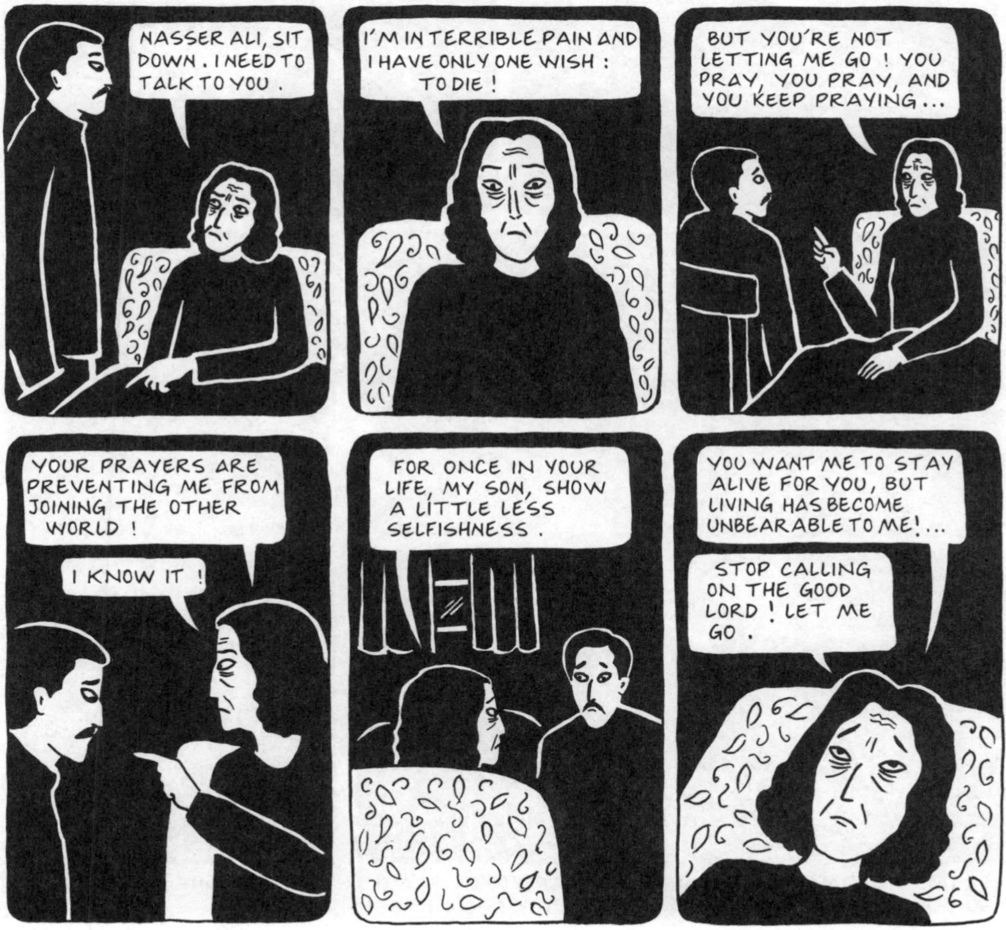
NASSER ALI, SIT DOWN . I NEED TO TALK TO YOU .
I'M IN TERRIBLE PAIN AND I HAVE ONLY ONE WISH : TO DIE !
BUT YOU'RE NOT LETTING ME GO ! YOU PRAY, YOU PRAY, AND YOU KEEP PRAYING...
YOUR PRAYERS ARE PREVENTING ME FROM JOINING THE OTHER WORLD !
I KNOW IT !
FOR ONCE IN YOUR LIFE, MY SON, SHOW A LITTLE LESS SELFISHNESS .
YOU WANT ME TO STAY ALIVE FOR YOU, BUT LIVING HAS BECOME UNBEARABLE TO ME!...
STOP CALLING ON THE GOOD LORD ! LET ME GO .

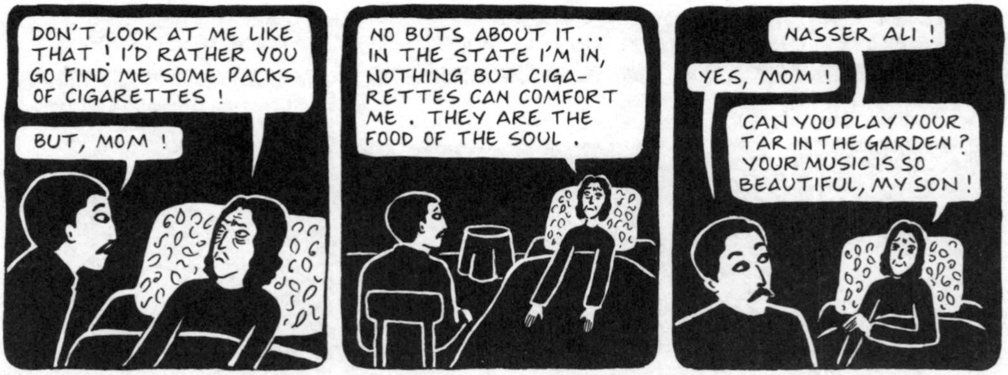
DON'T LOOK AT ME LIKE THAT ! I'D RATHER YOU GO FIND ME SOME PACKS OF CIGARETTES !
BUT, MOM !
NO BUTS ABOUT IT... IN THE STATE I'M IN, NOTHING BUT CIGA-RETTES CAN COMFORT ME . THEY ARE THE FOOD OF THE SOUL .
NASSER ALI !
YES, MOM !
CAN YOU PLAY YOUR TAR IN THE GARDEN ? YOUR MUSIC IS SO BEAUTIFUL, MY SON !

NASSER ALI KHAN OBEYED . HE BOUGHT THREE DOZEN PACKS OF CIGARETTES AND HANDED THEM OVER TO HIS MOTHER . HE NO LONGER PRAYED FOR HER AND HE PLAYED MUSIC EVERY DAY, FROM SUNRISE TO THE STROKE OF MIDNIGHT .

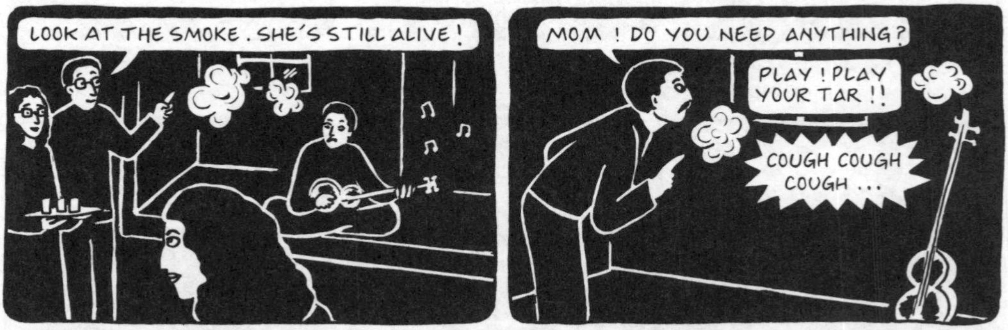
LOOK AT THE SMOKE . SHE'S STILL ALIVE !
MOM ! DO YOU NEED ANYTHING ?
PLAY ! PLAY YOUR TAR !!
COUGH COUGH COUGH ...

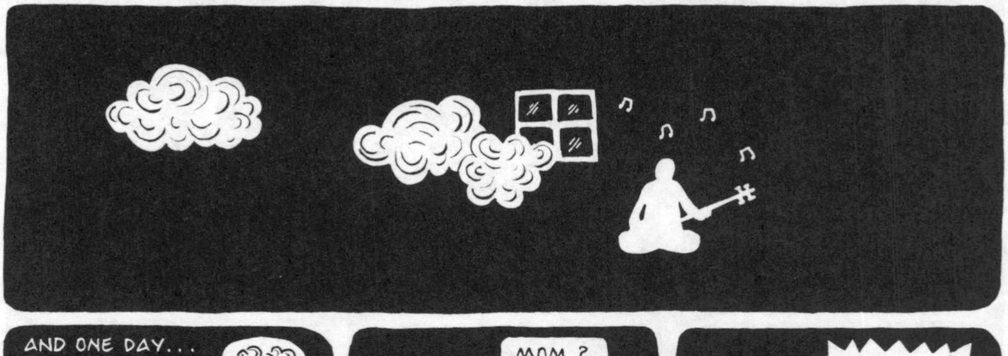

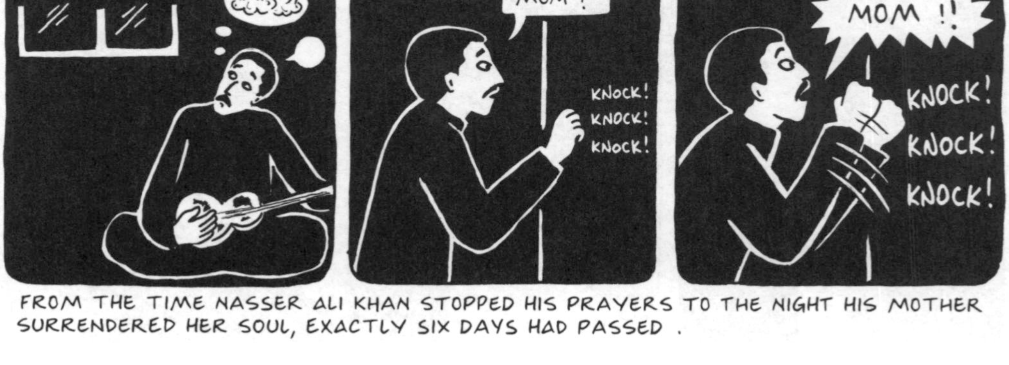
AND ONE DAY...
MOM ?
KNOCK!
KNOCK!
KNOCK!
MOM !!
KNOCK!
KNOCK!
KNOCK!

FROM THE TIME NASSER ALI KHAN STOPPED HIS PRAYERS TO THE NIGHT HIS MOTHER SURRENDERED HER SOUL, EXACTLY SIX DAYS HAD PASSED .

IT SEEMS THAT WHEN THEY DISCOVERED HER BODY, IT WAS ENVELOPED IN A THICK CLOUD OF SMOKE.

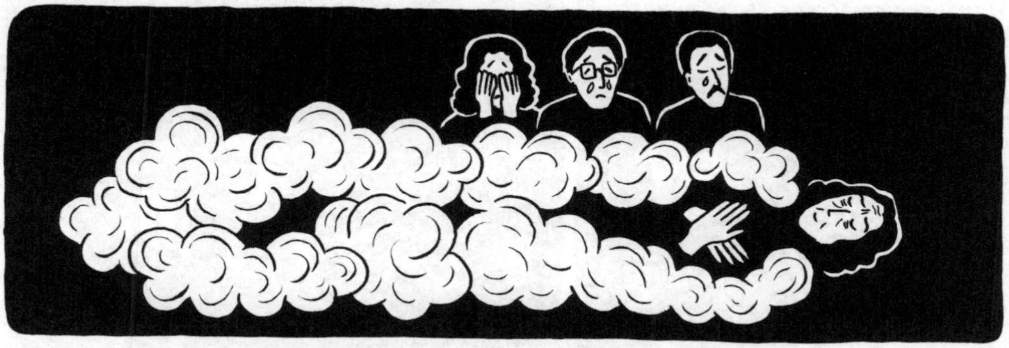

THE FUNERAL TOOK PLACE TWO DAYS LATER. THE FAMILY OF THE DECEASED, ALL THE DERVISHES* OF TEHRAN, AS WELL AS THE CLOUD OF SMOKE WERE PRESENT AT THE BURIAL.

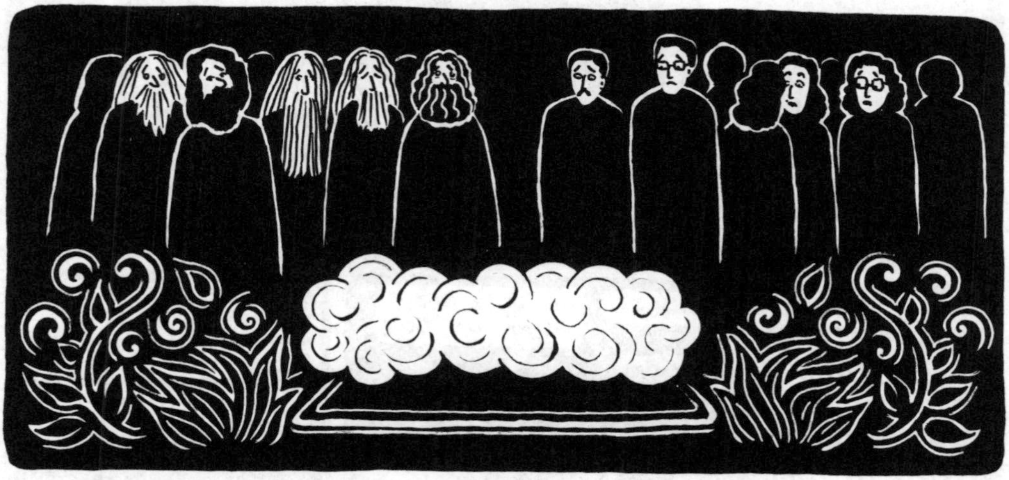

THE OPINIONS ON THIS DENSE FOG WERE VERY DIVERGENT:
THE RATIONAL ONES THOUGHT THAT IT WAS THE CIGARETTE SMOKE LEAVING HER BODY. HAVING SAID THIS, THEY WERE NEVER ABLE TO EXPLAIN SCIENTIFICALLY HOW A CADAVER COULD CONTINUE TO EXHALE.
THE DERVISHES, MORE MYSTICAL, HAD A COMPLETELY DIFFERENT OPINION ON THIS SUBJECT:

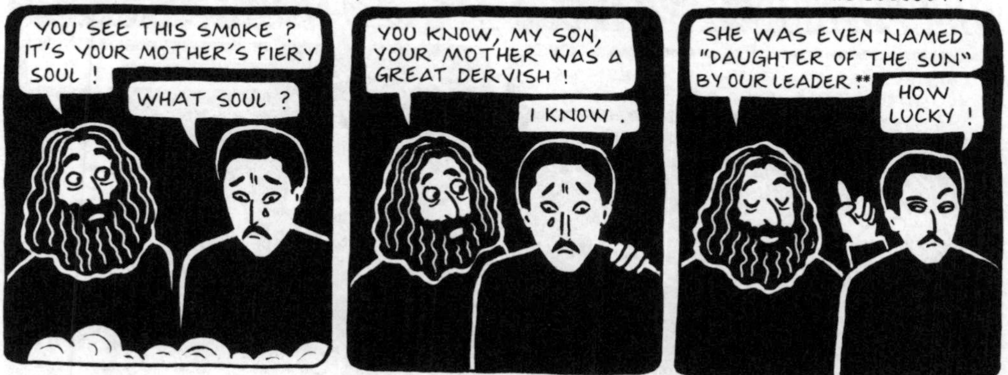
YOU SEE THIS SMOKE? IT'S YOUR MOTHER'S FIERY SOUL!
WHAT SOUL?
YOU KNOW, MY SON, YOUR MOTHER WAS A GREAT DERVISH!
I KNOW.
SHE WAS EVEN NAMED "DAUGHTER OF THE SUN" BY OUR LEADER**
HOW LUCKY!

*SUFI MYSTICS. ** HEAD OF THE DERVISHES ("GHOTB" IN PERSIAN).

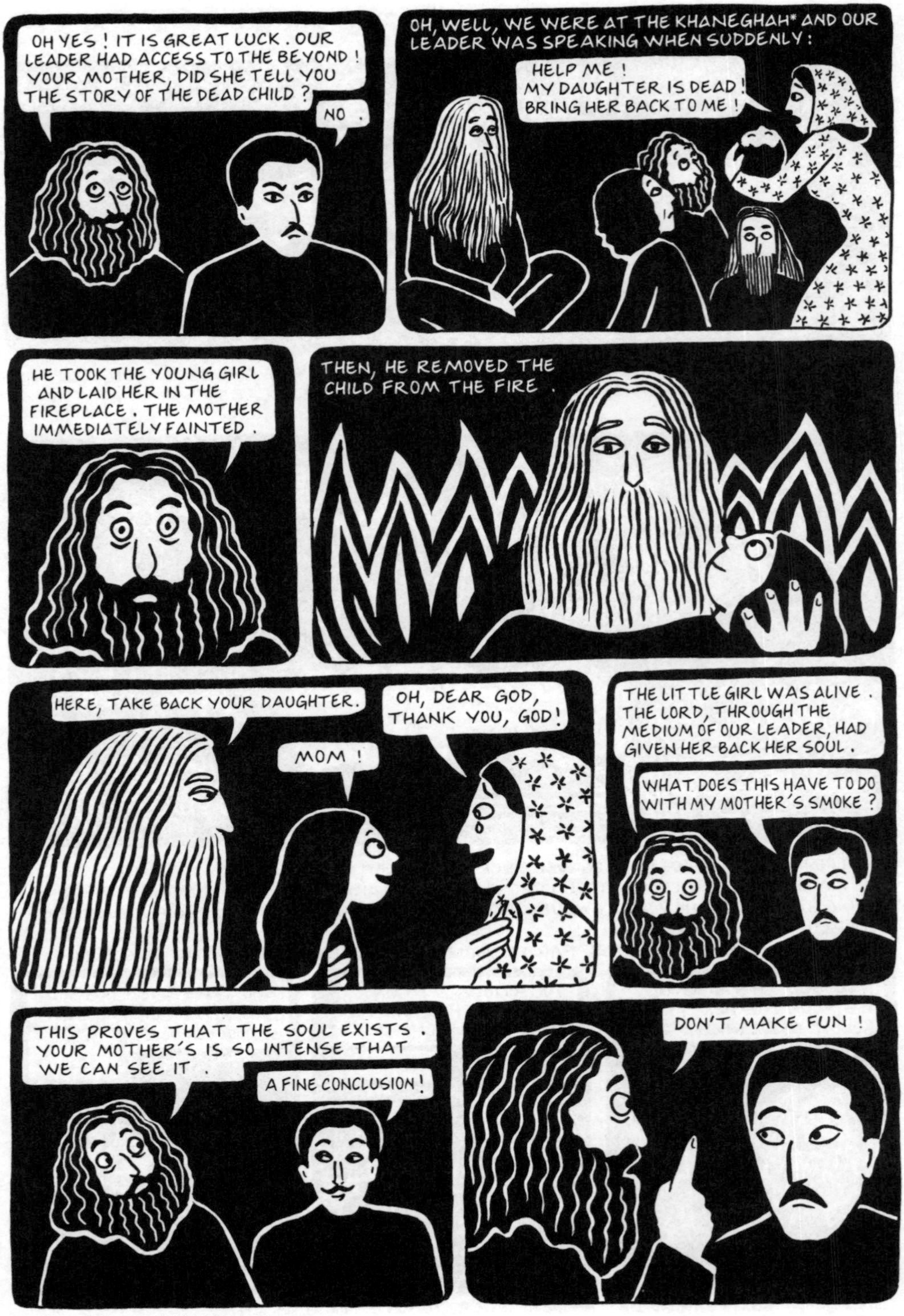

OH YES! IT IS GREAT LUCK. OUR LEADER HAD ACCESS TO THE BEYOND! YOUR MOTHER, DID SHE TELL YOU THE STORY OF THE DEAD CHILD?
NO.
OH, WELL, WE WERE AT THE KHANEGHAH* AND OUR LEADER WAS SPEAKING WHEN SUDDENLY:
HELP ME! MY DAUGHTER IS DEAD! BRING HER BACK TO ME!
HE TOOK THE YOUNG GIRL AND LAID HER IN THE FIREPLACE. THE MOTHER IMMEDIATELY FAINTED.
THEN, HE REMOVED THE CHILD FROM THE FIRE.
HERE, TAKE BACK YOUR DAUGHTER.
MOM!
OH, DEAR GOD, THANK YOU, GOD!
THE LITTLE GIRL WAS ALIVE. THE LORD, THROUGH THE MEDIUM OF OUR LEADER, HAD GIVEN HER BACK HER SOUL.
WHAT DOES THIS HAVE TO DO WITH MY MOTHER'S SMOKE?
THIS PROVES THAT THE SOUL EXISTS. YOUR MOTHER'S IS SO INTENSE THAT WE CAN SEE IT.
A FINE CONCLUSION!
DON'T MAKE FUN!

*THE DERVISHES' MOSQUE.

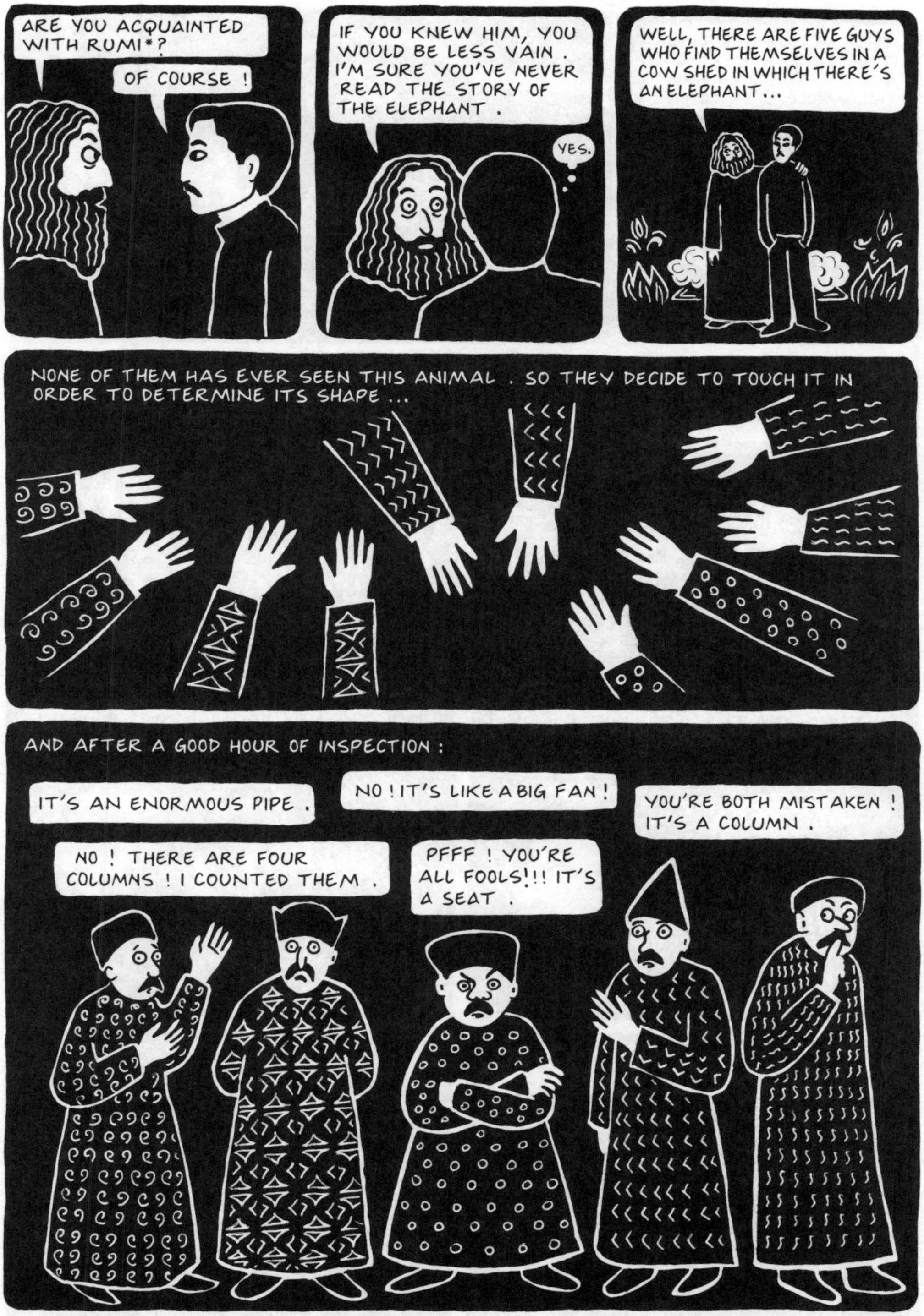
ARE YOU ACQUAINTED WITH RUMI*?
OF COURSE !
IF YOU KNEW HIM, YOU WOULD BE LESS VAIN . I'M SURE YOU'VE NEVER READ THE STORY OF THE ELEPHANT .
YES.
WELL, THERE ARE FIVE GUYS WHO FIND THEMSELVES IN A COW SHED IN WHICH THERE'S AN ELEPHANT...
NONE OF THEM HAS EVER SEEN THIS ANIMAL . SO THEY DECIDE TO TOUCH IT IN ORDER TO DETERMINE ITS SHAPE ...
AND AFTER A GOOD HOUR OF INSPECTION :
IT'S AN ENORMOUS PIPE .
NO ! IT'S LIKE A BIG FAN !
YOU'RE BOTH MISTAKEN ! IT'S A COLUMN .
NO ! THERE ARE FOUR COLUMNS ! I COUNTED THEM .
PFFF ! YOU'RE ALL FOOLS!!! IT'S A SEAT .

*IRANIAN POET (1207-1273). BARD OF MYSTICAL LOVE AND FOUNDER OF THE MOWLAVI ORDER OF SUFIS (KNOWN AS WHIRLING DERVISHES).

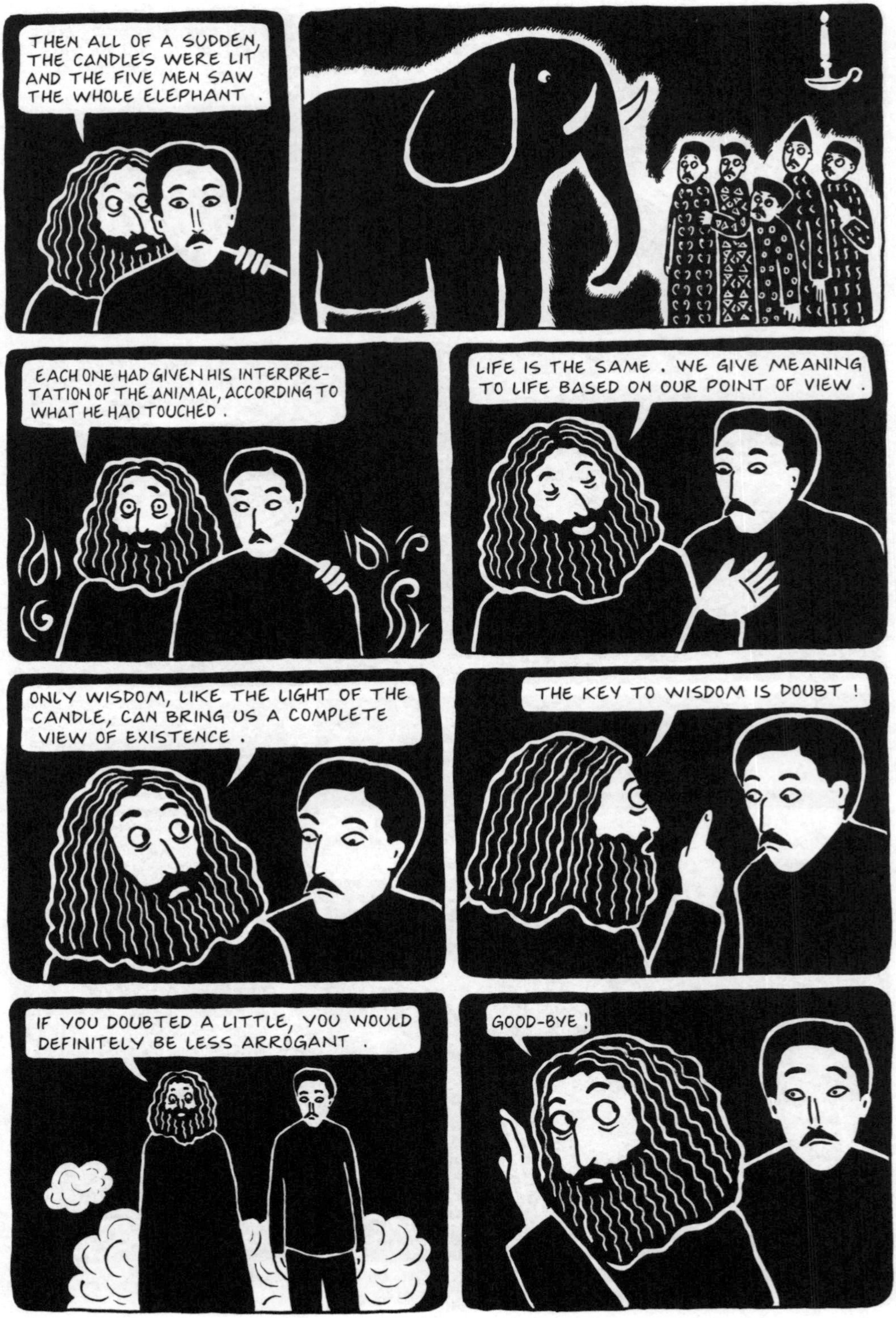
THEN ALL OF A SUDDEN, THE CANDLES WERE LIT AND THE FIVE MEN SAW THE WHOLE ELEPHANT.
EACH ONE HAD GIVEN HIS INTERPRETATION OF THE ANIMAL, ACCORDING TO WHAT HE HAD TOUCHED.
LIFE IS THE SAME. WE GIVE MEANING TO LIFE BASED ON OUR POINT OF VIEW.
ONLY WISDOM, LIKE THE LIGHT OF THE CANDLE, CAN BRING US A COMPLETE VIEW OF EXISTENCE.
THE KEY TO WISDOM IS DOUBT!
IF YOU DOUBTED A LITTLE, YOU WOULD DEFINITELY BE LESS ARROGANT.
GOOD-BYE!

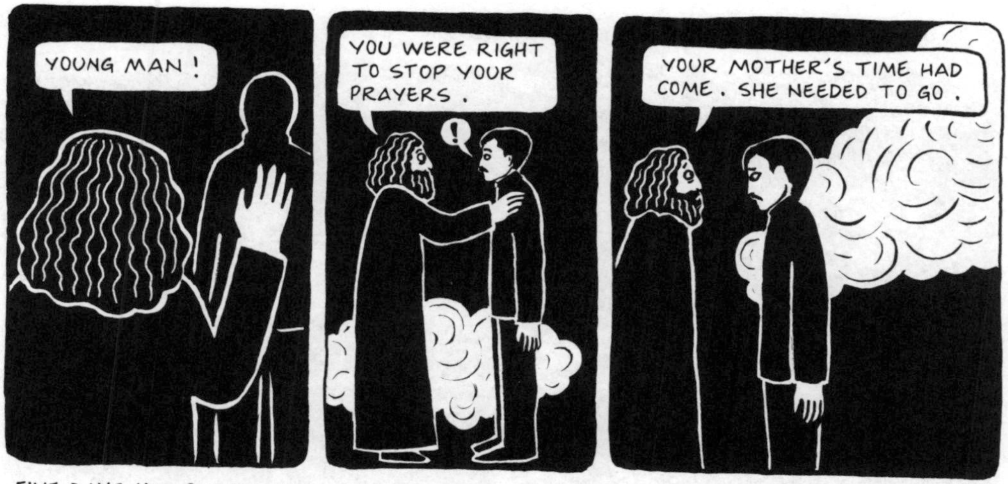
YOUNG MAN !
YOU WERE RIGHT TO STOP YOUR PRAYERS .
!
YOUR MOTHER'S TIME HAD COME . SHE NEEDED TO GO .

FIVE DAYS HAD PASSED AND NASSER ALI KHAN WAS ASKING HIMSELF MANY QUESTIONS :

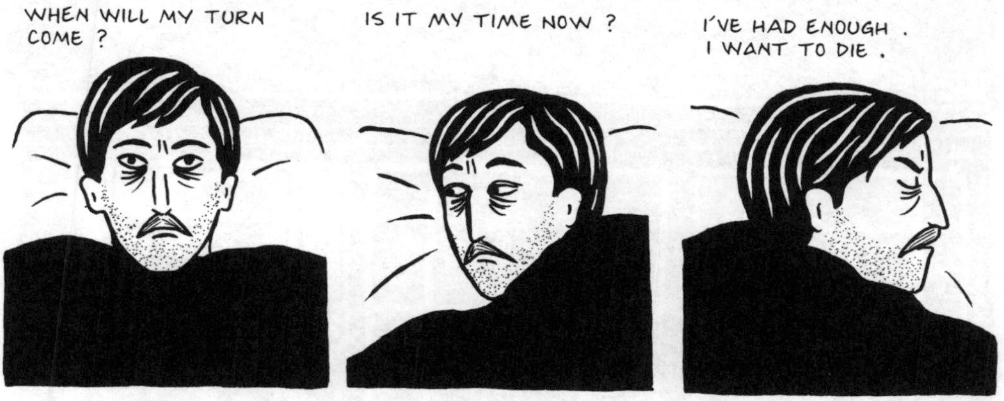
WHEN WILL MY TURN COME ?
IS IT MY TIME NOW ?
I'VE HAD ENOUGH . I WANT TO DIE .

HE CONCLUDED THAT IF DEATH WASN'T KEEPING THEIR APPOINTMENT, IT WAS BECAUSE SOMEONE WAS PRAYING FOR HIM TO GO ON LIVING .

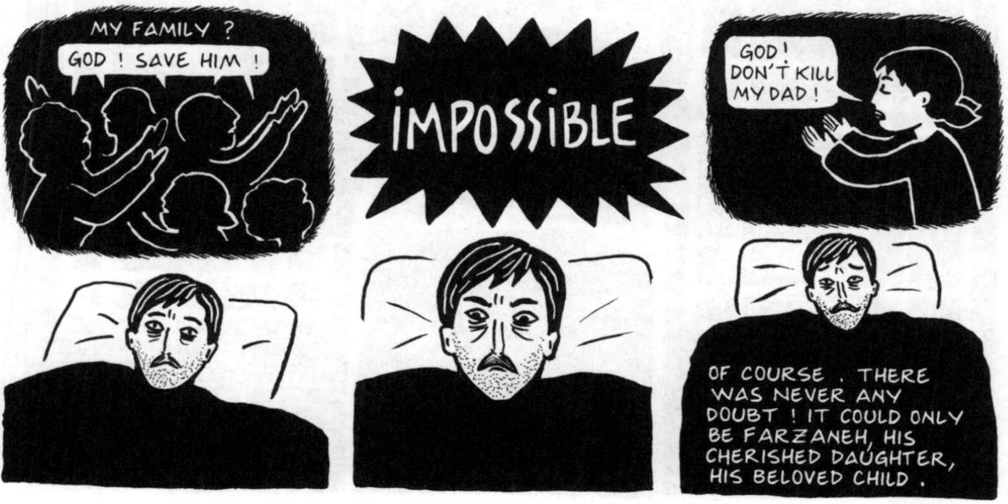
MY FAMILY ?
GOD ! SAVE HIM !
IMPOSSIBLE
GOD ! DON'T KILL MY DAD !
OF COURSE . THERE WAS NEVER ANY DOUBT ! IT COULD ONLY BE FARZANEH, HIS CHERISHED DAUGHTER, HIS BELOVED CHILD .

THE NIGHT OF NOVEMBER 19, 1958, A DARK SILENCE REIGNED OVER THE HOUSE.

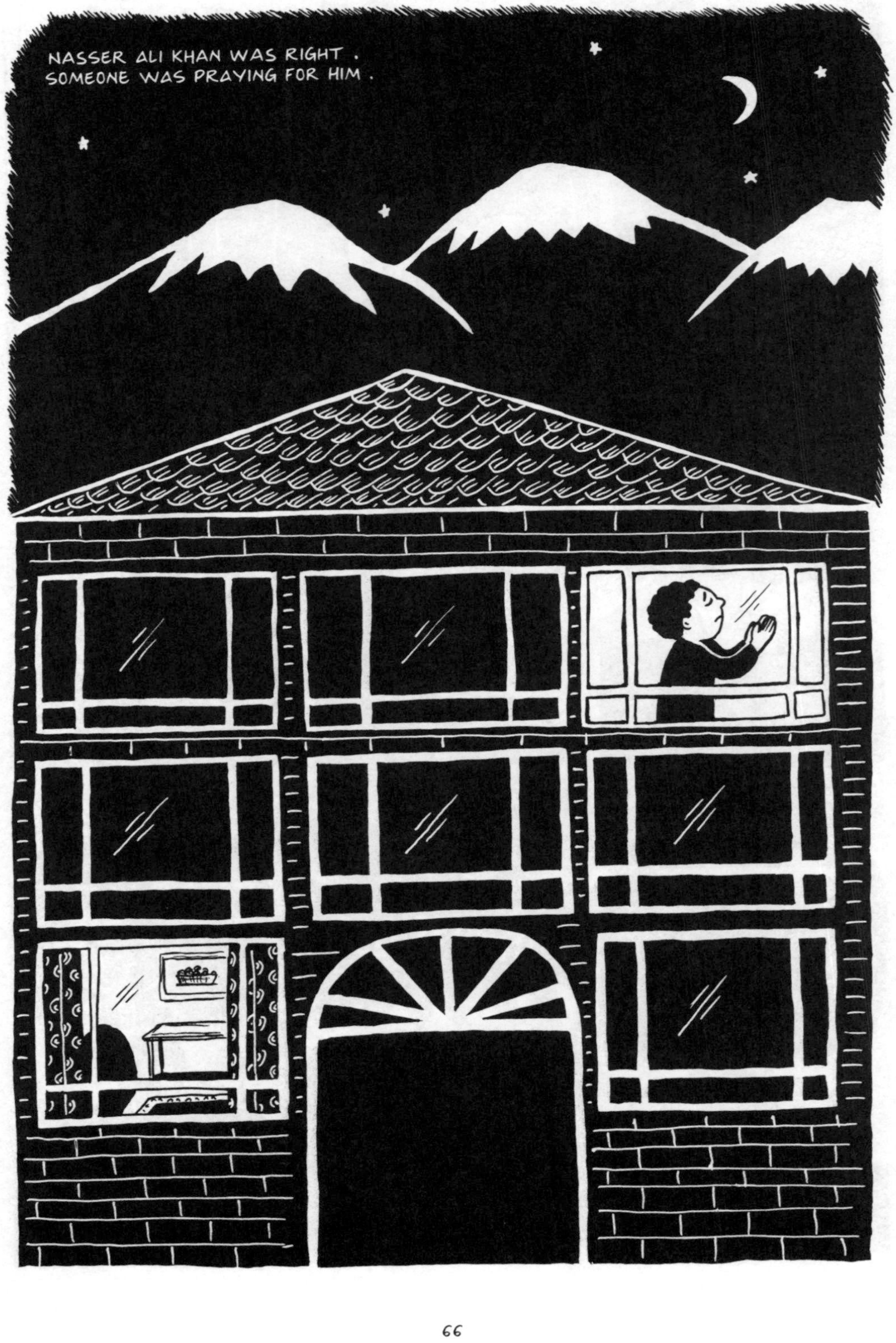
NASSER ALI KHAN WAS RIGHT. SOMEONE WAS PRAYING FOR HIM.

THE SIXTH DAY

NOVEMBER 20, 1958

IN THE COURSE OF THE SIXTH DAY, NASSER ALI KHAN FINALLY SAW AZRAEL, THE ANGEL OF DEATH. EVEN THOUGH HE WAS ANXIOUS TO LEAVE THIS WORLD, HE WAS VERY, VERY SCARED.

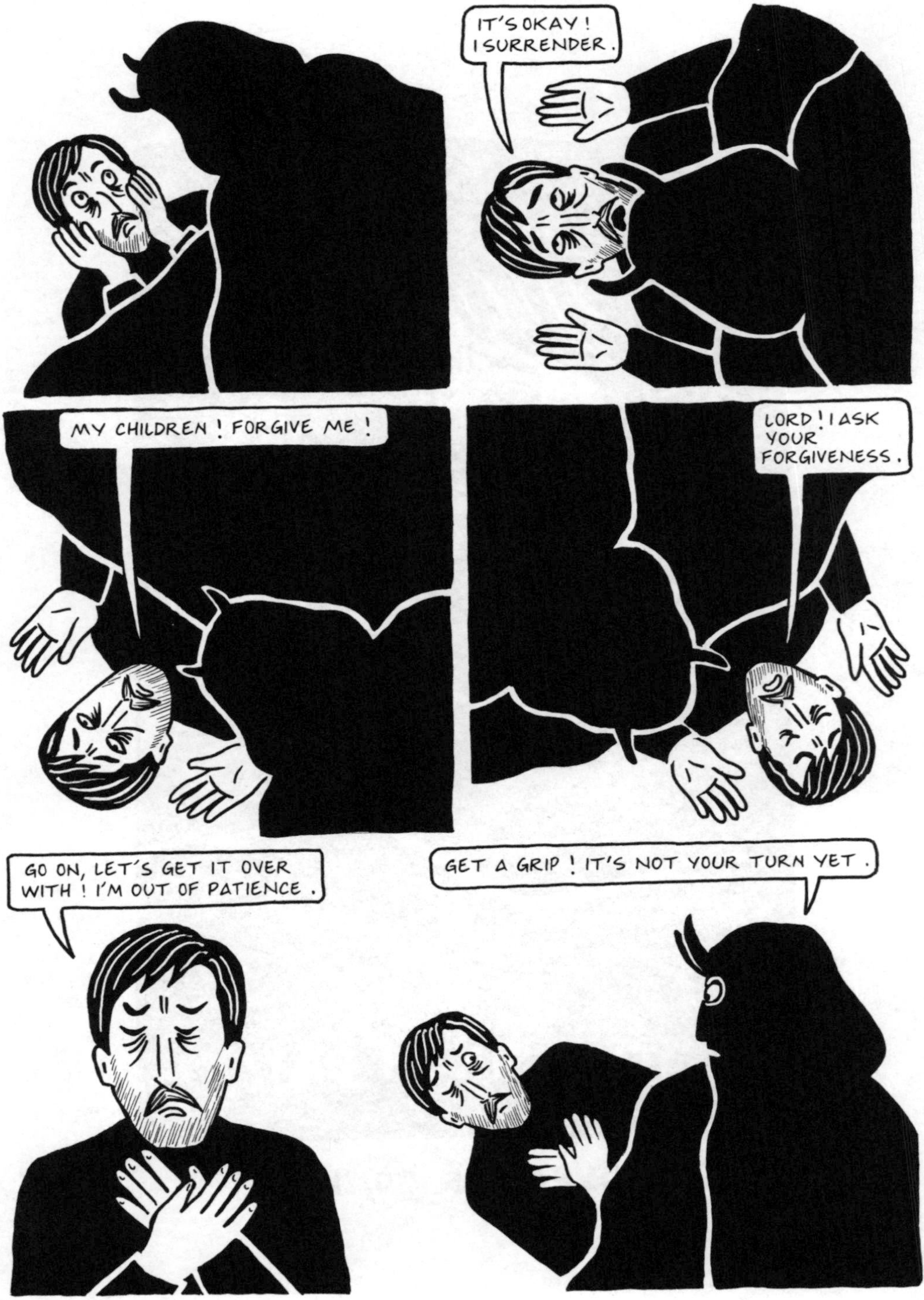

IT'S OKAY! I SURRENDER.
MY CHILDREN! FORGIVE ME!
LORD! I ASK YOUR FORGIVENESS.
GO ON, LET'S GET IT OVER WITH! I'M OUT OF PATIENCE.
GET A GRIP! IT'S NOT YOUR TURN YET.

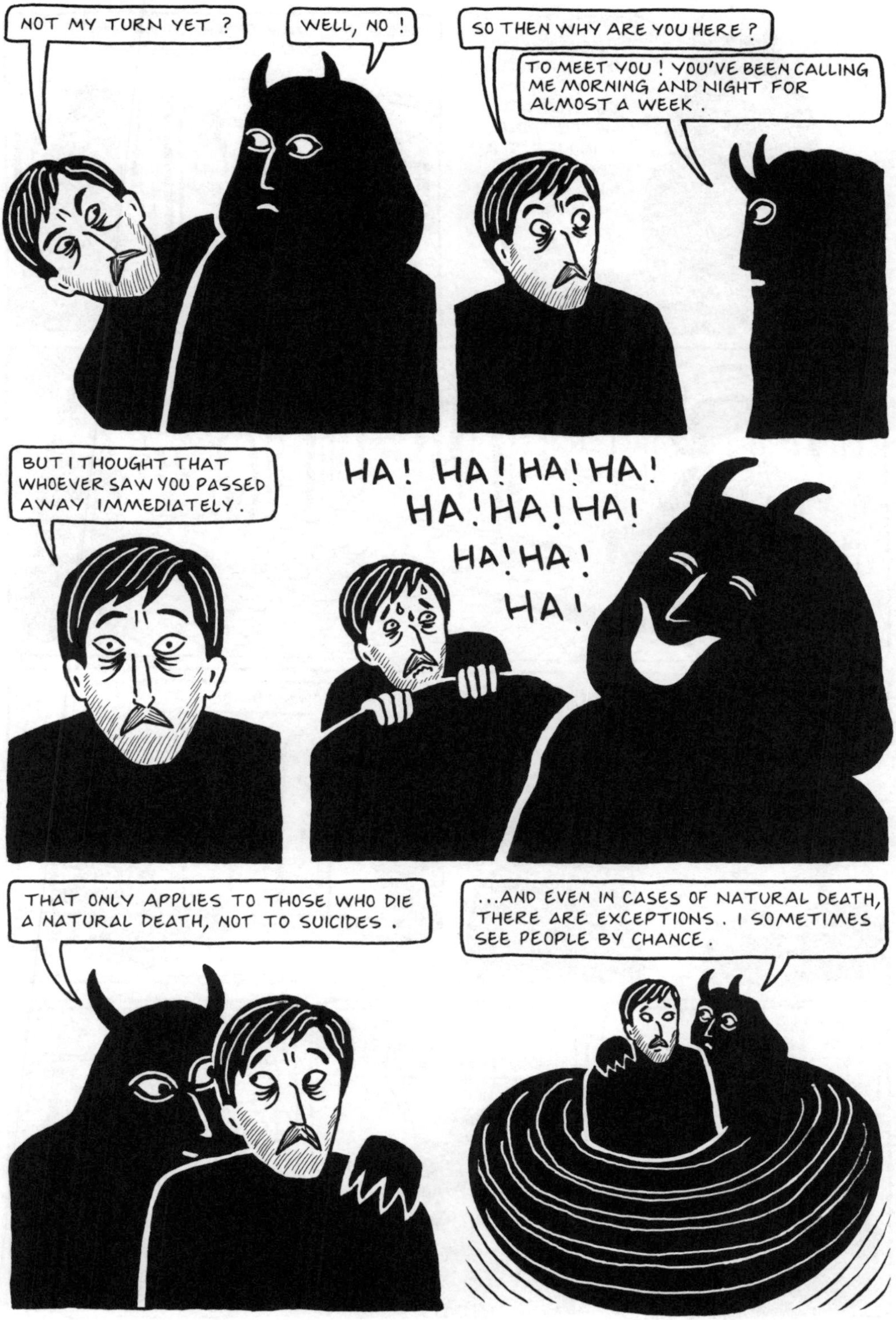
NOT MY TURN YET ?
WELL, NO !
SO THEN WHY ARE YOU HERE ?
TO MEET YOU ! YOU'VE BEEN CALLING ME MORNING AND NIGHT FOR ALMOST A WEEK .
BUT I THOUGHT THAT WHOEVER SAW YOU PASSED AWAY IMMEDIATELY .
HA! HA! HA! HA! HA! HA! HA! HA! HA! HA!
THAT ONLY APPLIES TO THOSE WHO DIE A NATURAL DEATH, NOT TO SUICIDES .
...AND EVEN IN CASES OF NATURAL DEATH, THERE ARE EXCEPTIONS . I SOMETIMES SEE PEOPLE BY CHANCE .

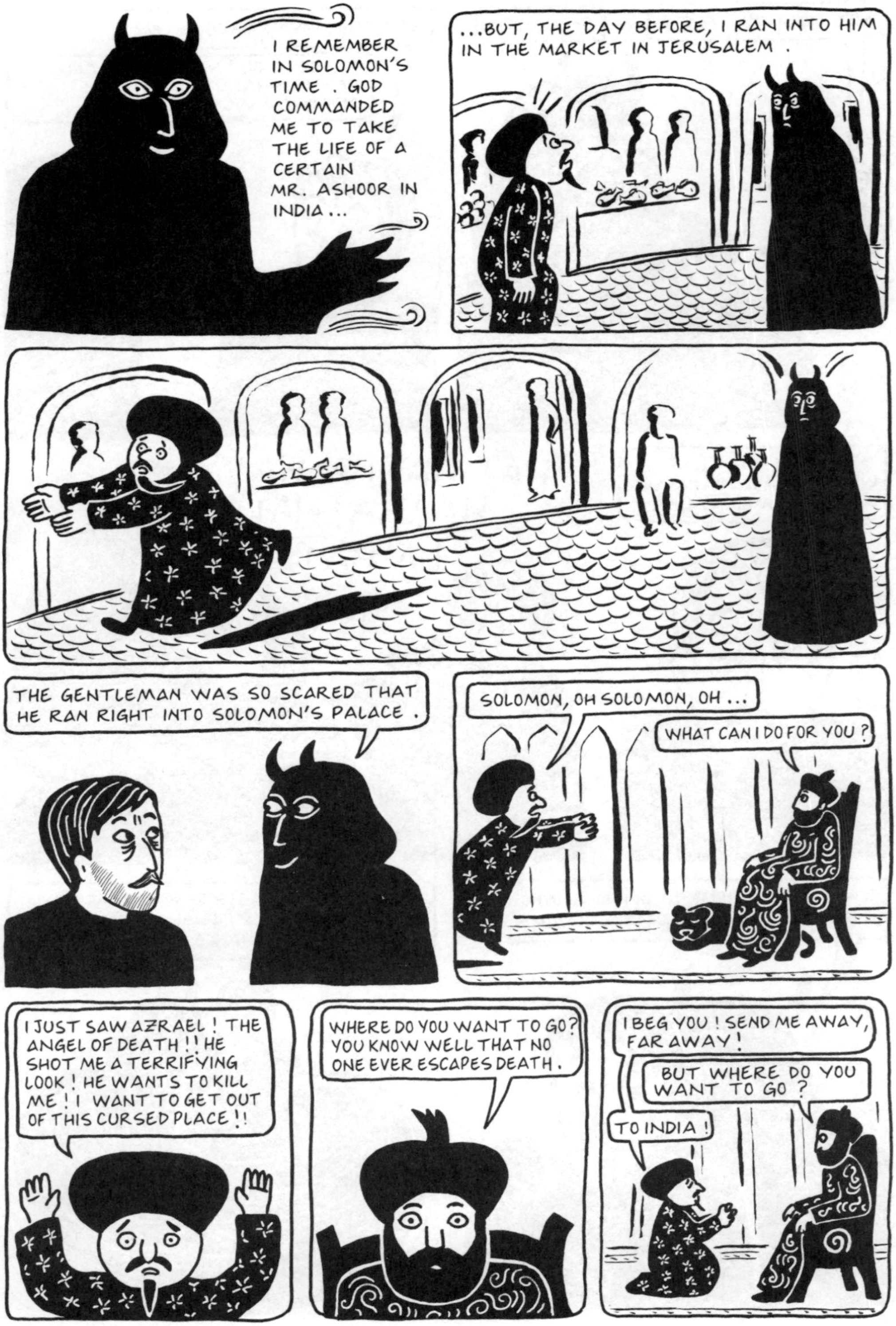
I REMEMBER IN SOLOMON'S TIME . GOD COMMANDED ME TO TAKE THE LIFE OF A CERTAIN MR. ASHOOR IN INDIA ...
...BUT, THE DAY BEFORE, I RAN INTO HIM IN THE MARKET IN JERUSALEM .
THE GENTLEMAN WAS SO SCARED THAT HE RAN RIGHT INTO SOLOMON'S PALACE .
SOLOMON, OH SOLOMON, OH ...
WHAT CAN I DO FOR YOU ?
I JUST SAW AZRAEL ! THE ANGEL OF DEATH !! HE SHOT ME A TERRIFYING LOOK ! HE WANTS TO KILL ME ! I WANT TO GET OUT OF THIS CURSED PLACE !!
WHERE DO YOU WANT TO GO ? YOU KNOW WELL THAT NO ONE EVER ESCAPES DEATH .
I BEG YOU ! SEND ME AWAY, FAR AWAY !
BUT WHERE DO YOU WANT TO GO ?
TO INDIA !

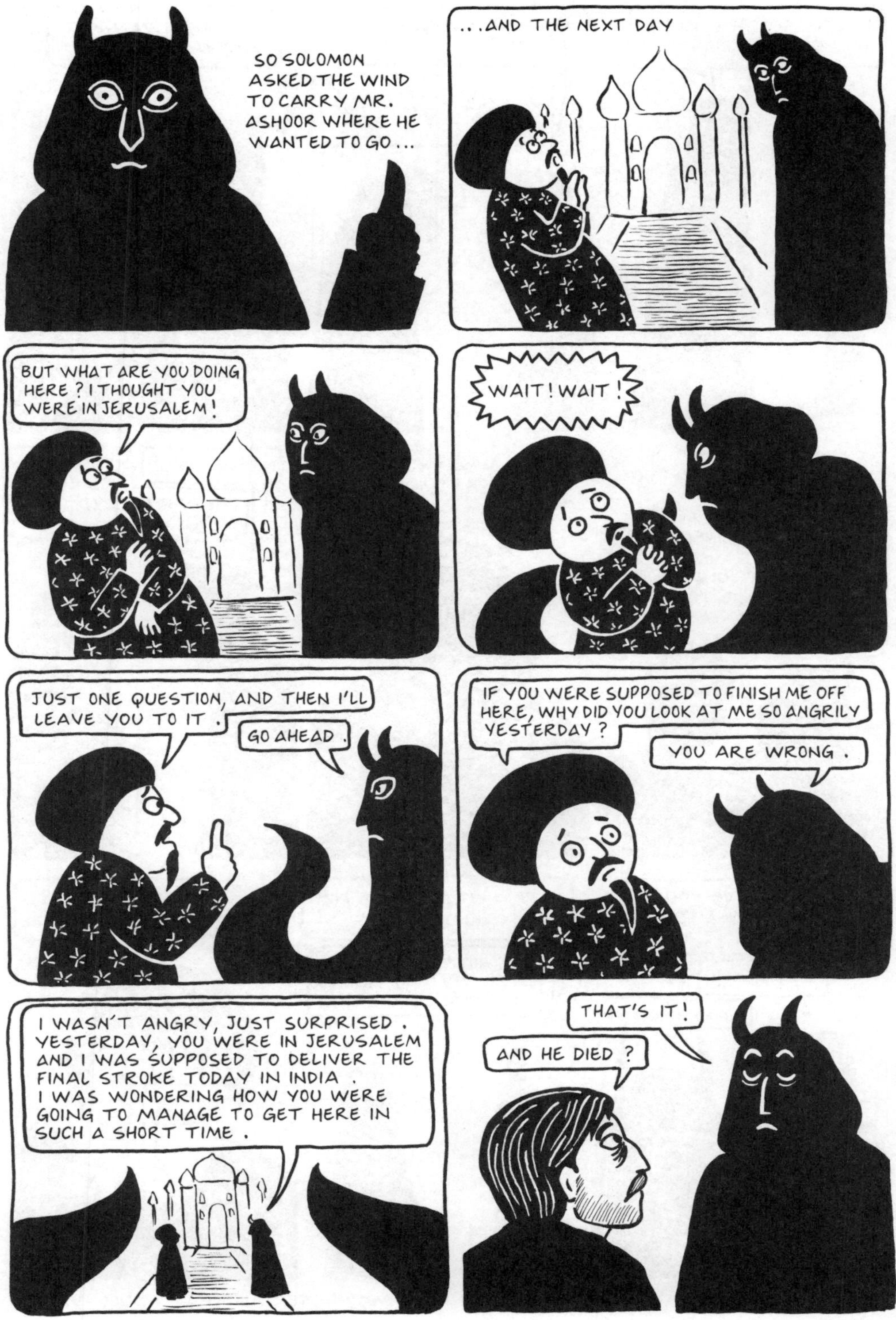

SO SOLOMON ASKED THE WIND TO CARRY MR. ASHOOR WHERE HE WANTED TO GO...
...AND THE NEXT DAY
BUT WHAT ARE YOU DOING HERE? I THOUGHT YOU WERE IN JERUSALEM!
WAIT! WAIT!
JUST ONE QUESTION, AND THEN I'LL LEAVE YOU TO IT.
GO AHEAD.
IF YOU WERE SUPPOSED TO FINISH ME OFF HERE, WHY DID YOU LOOK AT ME SO ANGRILY YESTERDAY?
YOU ARE WRONG.
I WASN'T ANGRY, JUST SURPRISED. YESTERDAY, YOU WERE IN JERUSALEM AND I WAS SUPPOSED TO DELIVER THE FINAL STROKE TODAY IN INDIA. I WAS WONDERING HOW YOU WERE GOING TO MANAGE TO GET HERE IN SUCH A SHORT TIME.
AND HE DIED?
THAT'S IT!

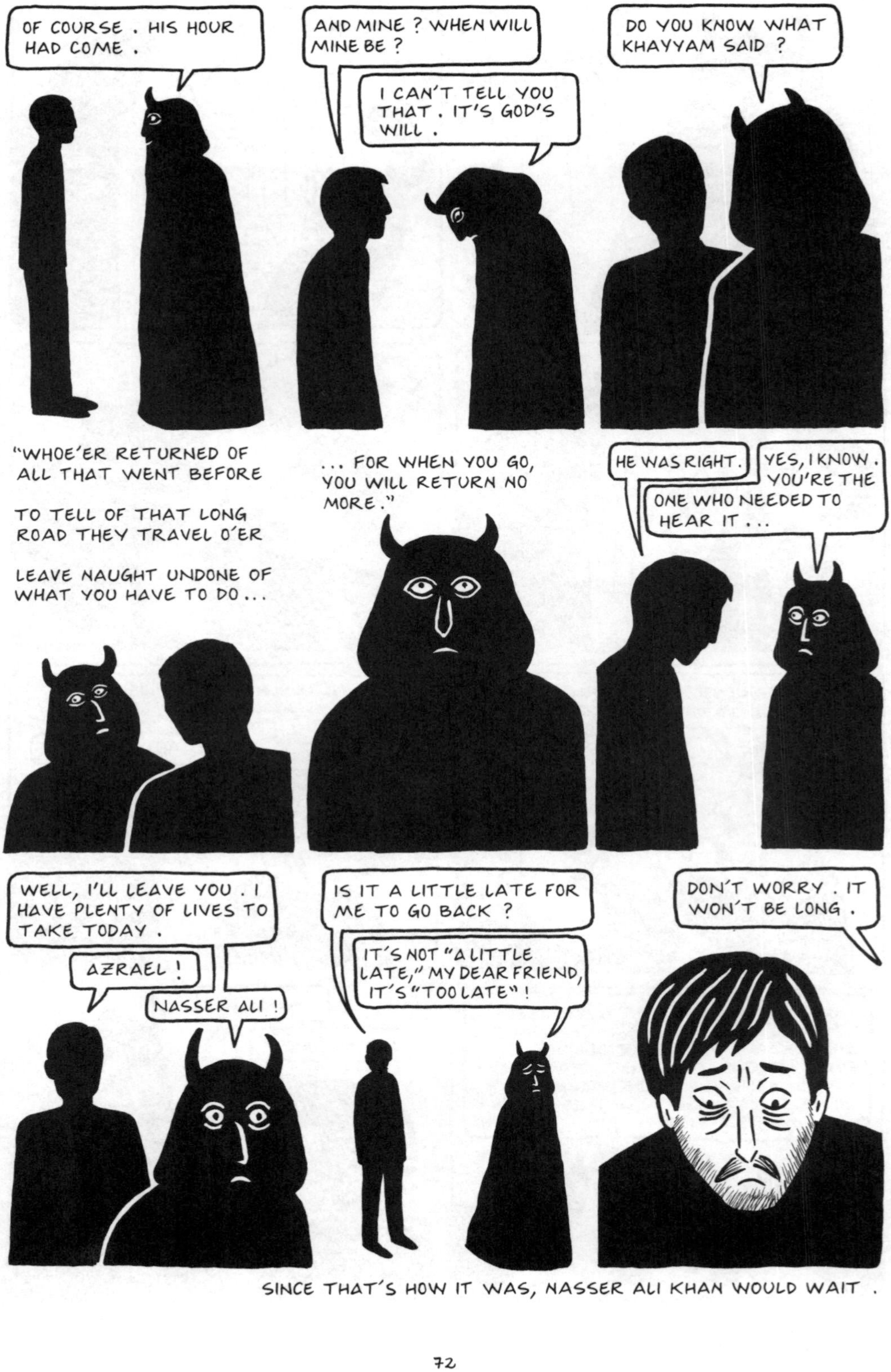

OF COURSE . HIS HOUR HAD COME .
AND MINE ? WHEN WILL MINE BE ?
I CAN'T TELL YOU THAT . IT'S GOD'S WILL .
DO YOU KNOW WHAT KHAYYAM SAID ?
"WHOE'ER RETURNED OF ALL THAT WENT BEFORE
TO TELL OF THAT LONG ROAD THEY TRAVEL O'ER
LEAVE NAUGHT UNDONE OF WHAT YOU HAVE TO DO...
... FOR WHEN YOU GO, YOU WILL RETURN NO MORE."
HE WAS RIGHT.
YES, I KNOW. YOU'RE THE ONE WHO NEEDED TO HEAR IT...
WELL, I'LL LEAVE YOU . I HAVE PLENTY OF LIVES TO TAKE TODAY .
AZRAEL !
NASSER ALI !
IS IT A LITTLE LATE FOR ME TO GO BACK ?
IT'S NOT "A LITTLE LATE," MY DEAR FRIEND, IT'S "TOO LATE" !
DON'T WORRY . IT WON'T BE LONG .
SINCE THAT'S HOW IT WAS, NASSER ALI KHAN WOULD WAIT .

THE SEVENTH DAY

NOVEMBER 21, 1958

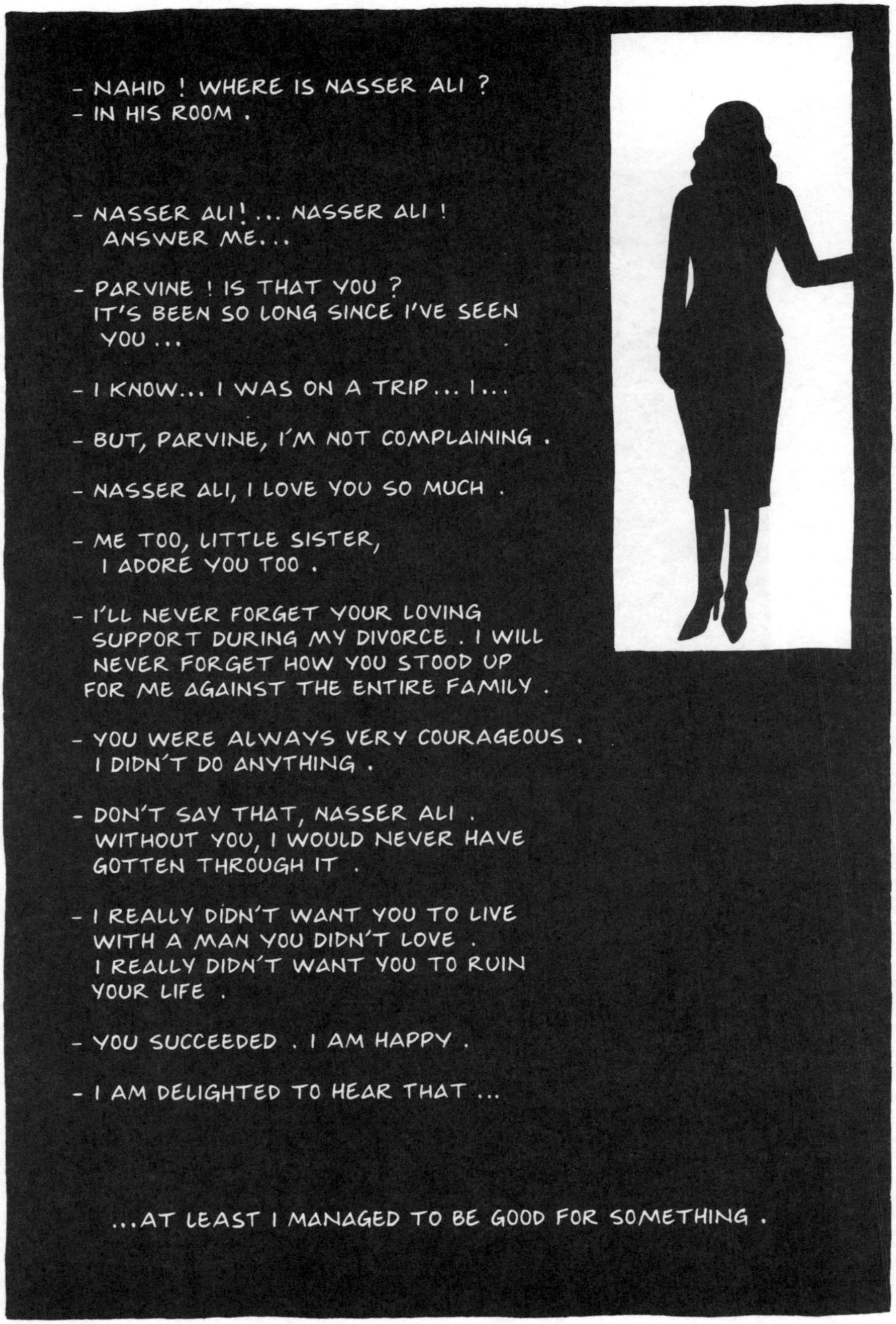
- NAHID ! WHERE IS NASSER ALI ?
- IN HIS ROOM .
- NASSER ALI ! ... NASSER ALI ! ANSWER ME...
- PARVINE ! IS THAT YOU ? IT'S BEEN SO LONG SINCE I'VE SEEN YOU ...
- I KNOW... I WAS ON A TRIP ... I ...
- BUT, PARVINE, I'M NOT COMPLAINING .
- NASSER ALI, I LOVE YOU SO MUCH .
- ME TOO, LITTLE SISTER, I ADORE YOU TOO .
- I'LL NEVER FORGET YOUR LOVING SUPPORT DURING MY DIVORCE . I WILL NEVER FORGET HOW YOU STOOD UP FOR ME AGAINST THE ENTIRE FAMILY .
- YOU WERE ALWAYS VERY COURAGEOUS . I DIDN'T DO ANYTHING .
- DON'T SAY THAT, NASSER ALI . WITHOUT YOU, I WOULD NEVER HAVE GOTTEN THROUGH IT .
- I REALLY DIDN'T WANT YOU TO LIVE WITH A MAN YOU DIDN'T LOVE . I REALLY DIDN'T WANT YOU TO RUIN YOUR LIFE .
- YOU SUCCEEDED . I AM HAPPY .
- I AM DELIGHTED TO HEAR THAT ...
...AT LEAST I MANAGED TO BE GOOD FOR SOMETHING .

THE EIGHTH DAY

NOVEMBER 22, 1958

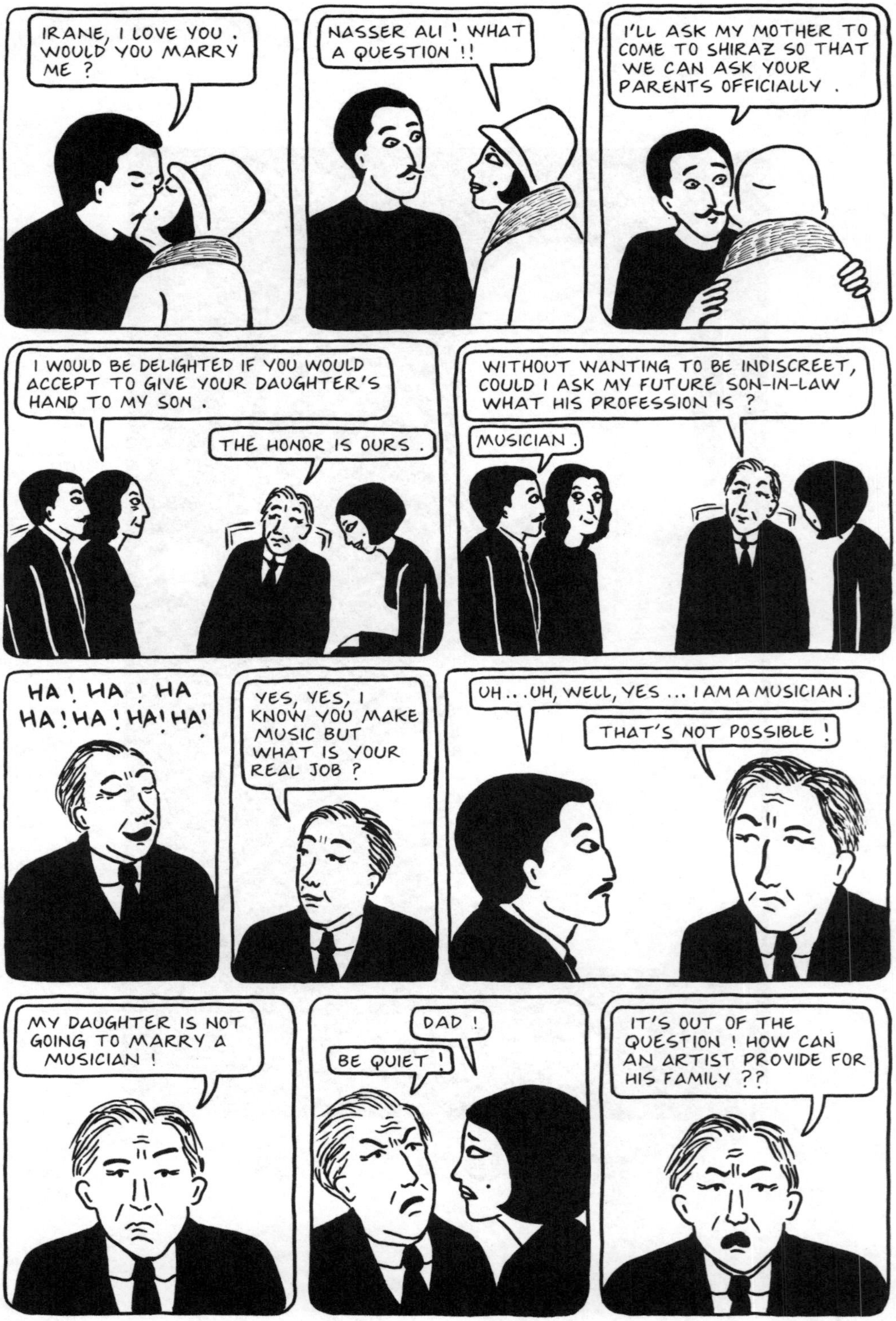
IRANE, I LOVE YOU. WOULD YOU MARRY ME?
NASSER ALI! WHAT A QUESTION!!
I'LL ASK MY MOTHER TO COME TO SHIRAZ SO THAT WE CAN ASK YOUR PARENTS OFFICIALLY.
I WOULD BE DELIGHTED IF YOU WOULD ACCEPT TO GIVE YOUR DAUGHTER'S HAND TO MY SON.
THE HONOR IS OURS.
WITHOUT WANTING TO BE INDISCREET, COULD I ASK MY FUTURE SON-IN-LAW WHAT HIS PROFESSION IS?
MUSICIAN.
HA! HA! HA HA! HA! HA! HA!
YES, YES, I KNOW YOU MAKE MUSIC BUT WHAT IS YOUR REAL JOB?
UH... UH, WELL, YES... I AM A MUSICIAN.
THAT'S NOT POSSIBLE!
MY DAUGHTER IS NOT GOING TO MARRY A MUSICIAN!
DAD!
BE QUIET!
IT'S OUT OF THE QUESTION! HOW CAN AN ARTIST PROVIDE FOR HIS FAMILY??

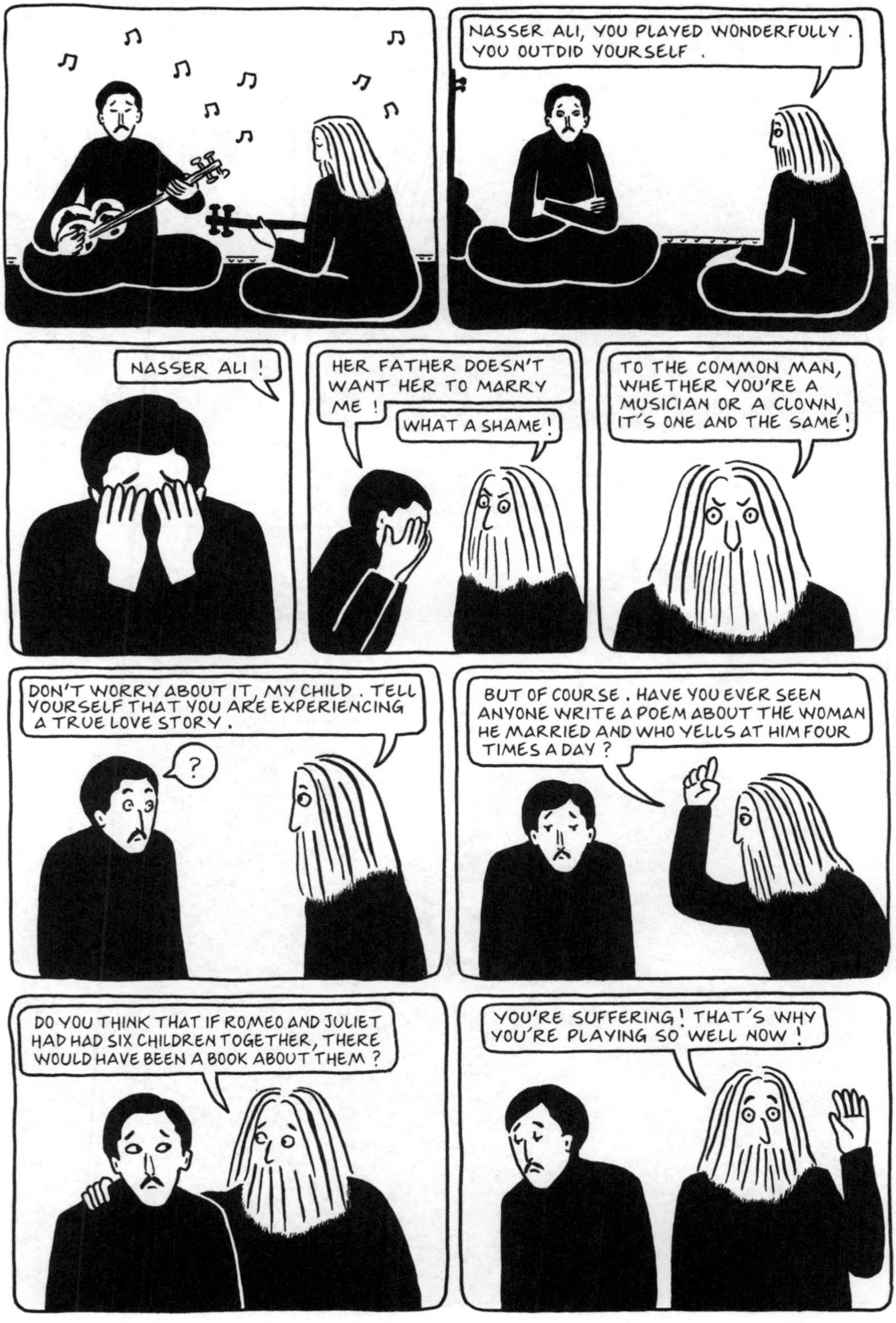
NASSER ALI, YOU PLAYED WONDERFULLY. YOU OUTDID YOURSELF.
NASSER ALI!
HER FATHER DOESN'T WANT HER TO MARRY ME!
WHAT A SHAME!
TO THE COMMON MAN, WHETHER YOU'RE A MUSICIAN OR A CLOWN, IT'S ONE AND THE SAME!
DON'T WORRY ABOUT IT, MY CHILD. TELL YOURSELF THAT YOU ARE EXPERIENCING A TRUE LOVE STORY.
?
BUT OF COURSE. HAVE YOU EVER SEEN ANYONE WRITE A POEM ABOUT THE WOMAN HE MARRIED AND WHO YELLS AT HIM FOUR TIMES A DAY?
DO YOU THINK THAT IF ROMEO AND JULIET HAD HAD SIX CHILDREN TOGETHER, THERE WOULD HAVE BEEN A BOOK ABOUT THEM?
YOU'RE SUFFERING! THAT'S WHY YOU'RE PLAYING SO WELL NOW!

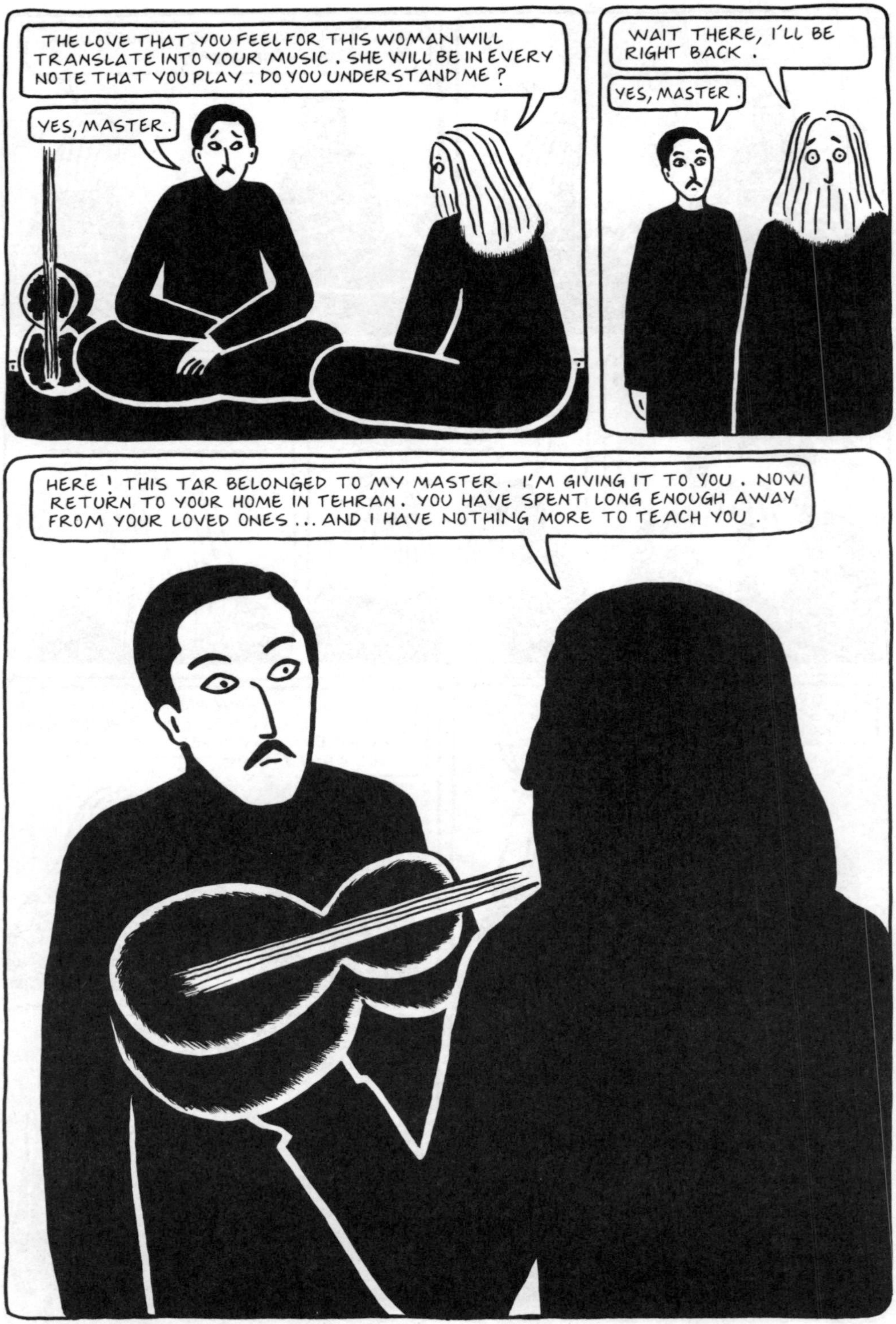
THE LOVE THAT YOU FEEL FOR THIS WOMAN WILL TRANSLATE INTO YOUR MUSIC. SHE WILL BE IN EVERY NOTE THAT YOU PLAY. DO YOU UNDERSTAND ME?
YES, MASTER.
WAIT THERE, I'LL BE RIGHT BACK.
YES, MASTER.
HERE! THIS TAR BELONGED TO MY MASTER. I'M GIVING IT TO YOU. NOW RETURN TO YOUR HOME IN TEHRAN. YOU HAVE SPENT LONG ENOUGH AWAY FROM YOUR LOVED ONES... AND I HAVE NOTHING MORE TO TEACH YOU.

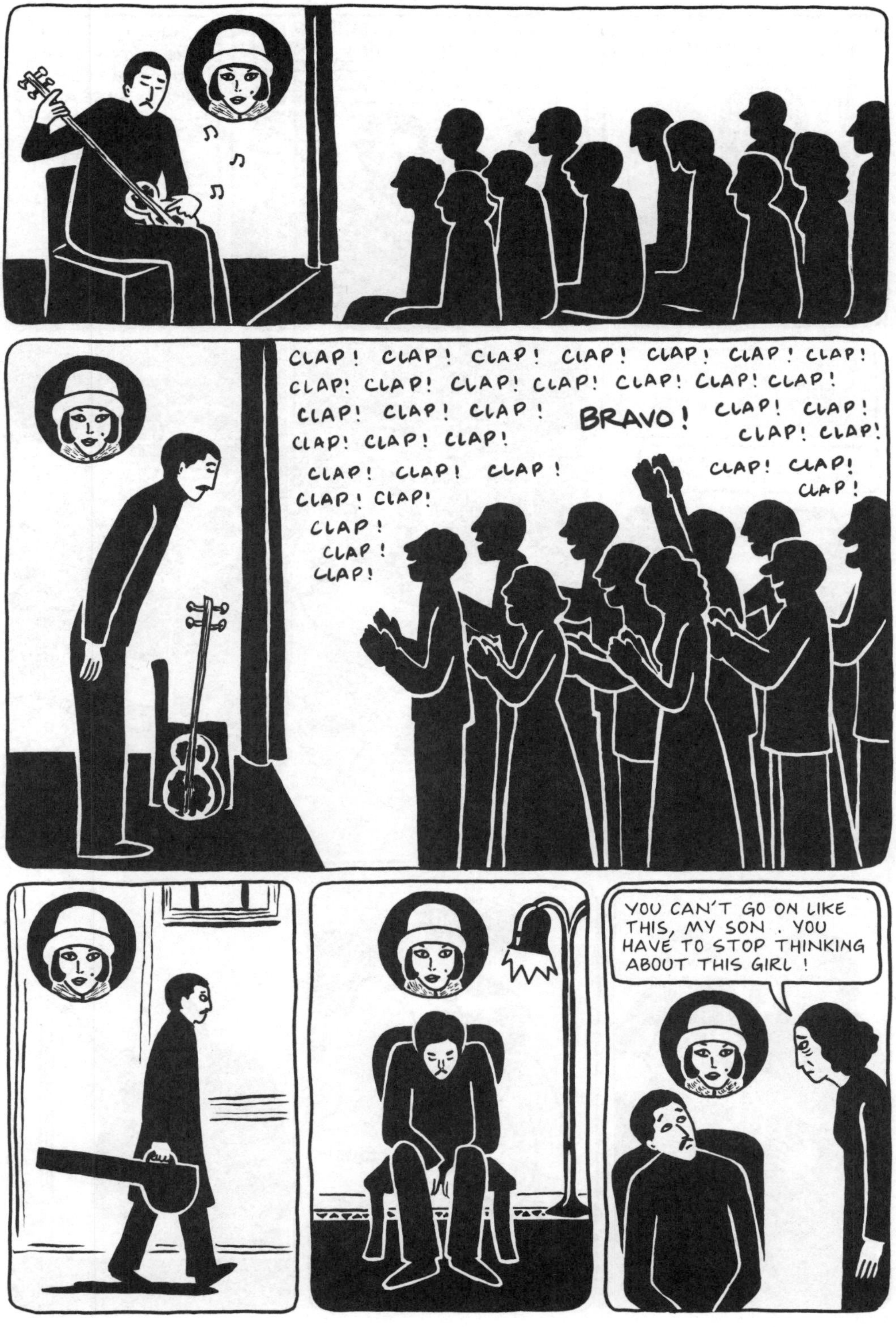
CLAP! CLAP! CLAP! CLAP! CLAP! CLAP! CLAP!
CLAP! CLAP! CLAP! CLAP! CLAP! CLAP! CLAP!
CLAP! CLAP! CLAP!
CLAP! CLAP! CLAP!
BRAVO!
CLAP! CLAP!
CLAP! CLAP!
CLAP! CLAP! CLAP!
CLAP! CLAP!
CLAP!
CLAP!
CLAP!
CLAP! CLAP!
CLAP!
YOU CAN'T GO ON LIKE THIS, MY SON . YOU HAVE TO STOP THINKING ABOUT THIS GIRL !

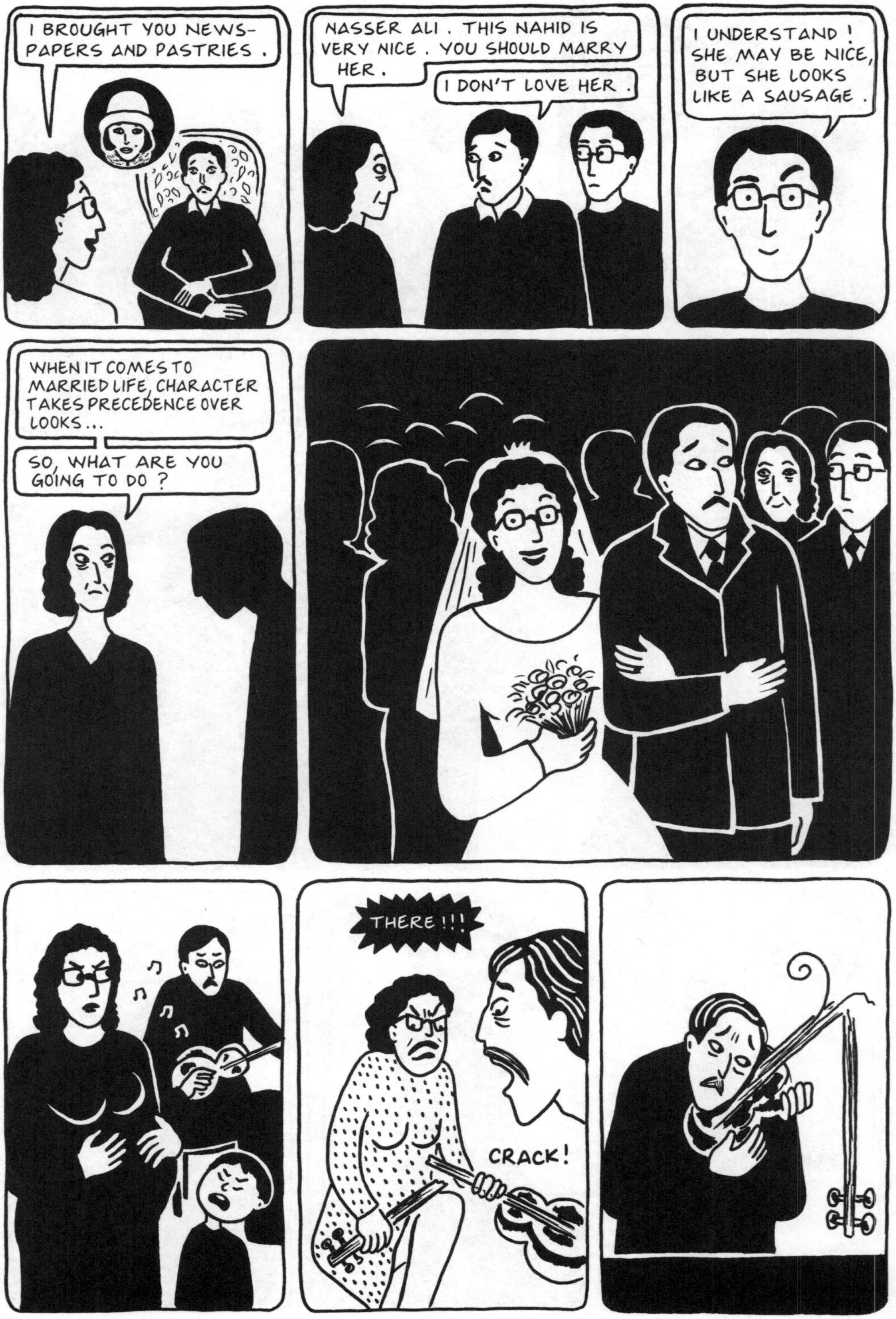

I BROUGHT YOU NEWSPAPERS AND PASTRIES .
NASSER ALI . THIS NAHID IS VERY NICE . YOU SHOULD MARRY HER .
I DON'T LOVE HER .
I UNDERSTAND ! SHE MAY BE NICE, BUT SHE LOOKS LIKE A SAUSAGE .
WHEN IT COMES TO MARRIED LIFE, CHARACTER TAKES PRECEDENCE OVER LOOKS...
SO, WHAT ARE YOU GOING TO DO ?
THERE !!!
CRACK!

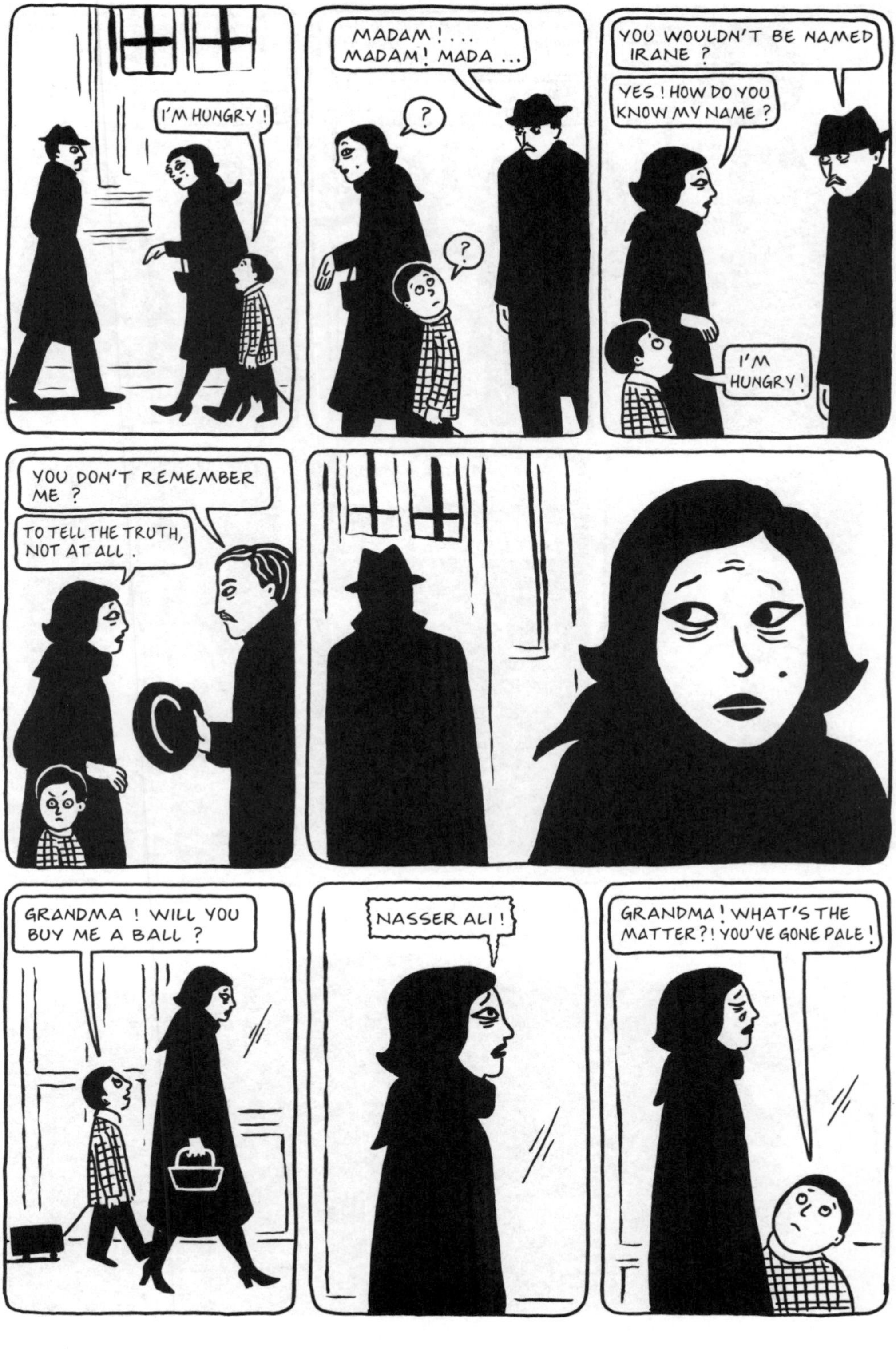
I'M HUNGRY!
MADAM!...
MADAM! MADA...
?
?
YOU WOULDN'T BE NAMED IRANE?
YES! HOW DO YOU KNOW MY NAME?
I'M HUNGRY!
YOU DON'T REMEMBER ME?
TO TELL THE TRUTH, NOT AT ALL.
GRANDMA! WILL YOU BUY ME A BALL?
NASSER ALI!
GRANDMA! WHAT'S THE MATTER?! YOU'VE GONE PALE!

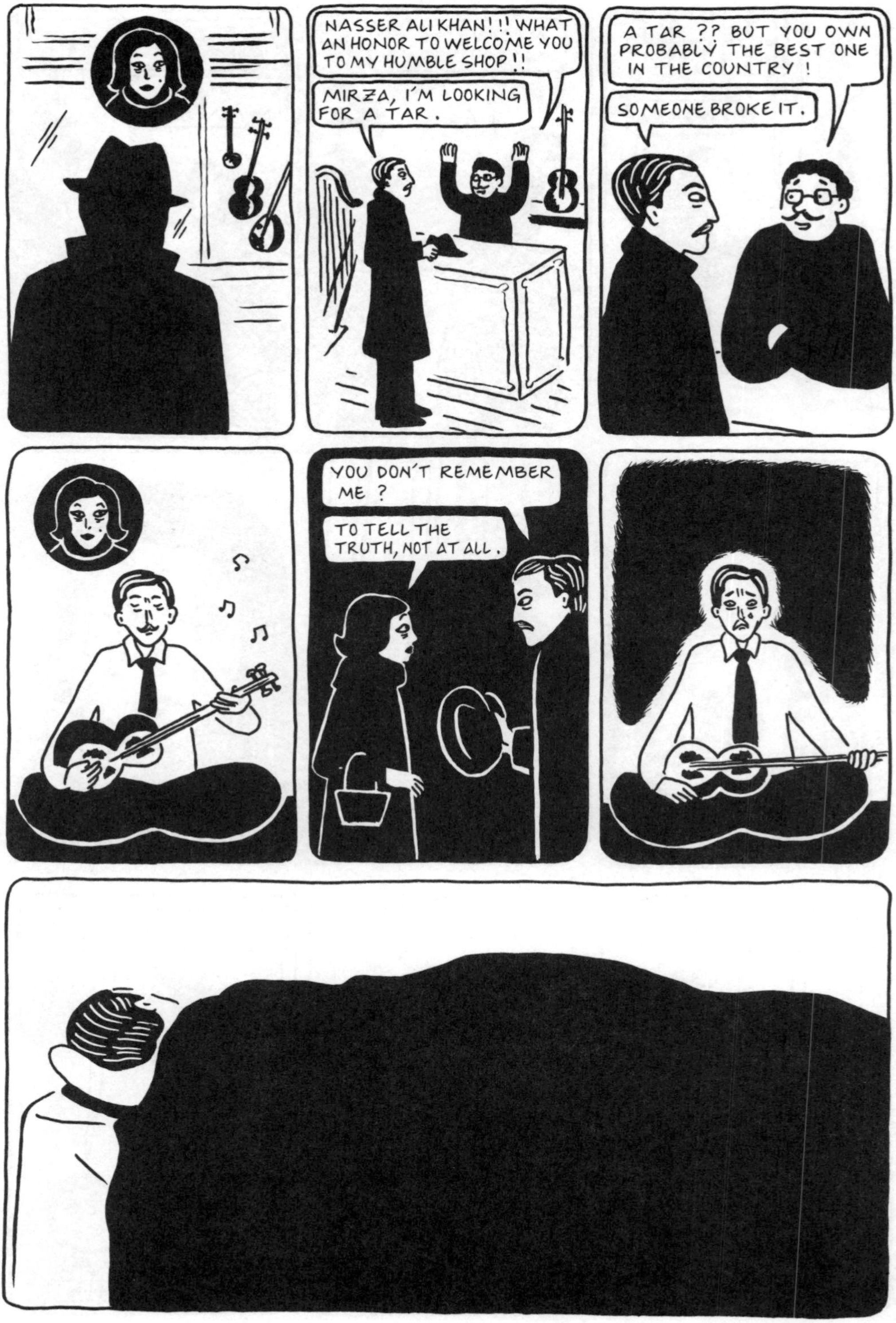
NASSER ALI KHAN!!! WHAT AN HONOR TO WELCOME YOU TO MY HUMBLE SHOP!!
MIRZA, I'M LOOKING FOR A TAR.
A TAR ?? BUT YOU OWN PROBABLY THE BEST ONE IN THE COUNTRY !
SOMEONE BROKE IT.
YOU DON'T REMEMBER ME ?
TO TELL THE TRUTH, NOT AT ALL.

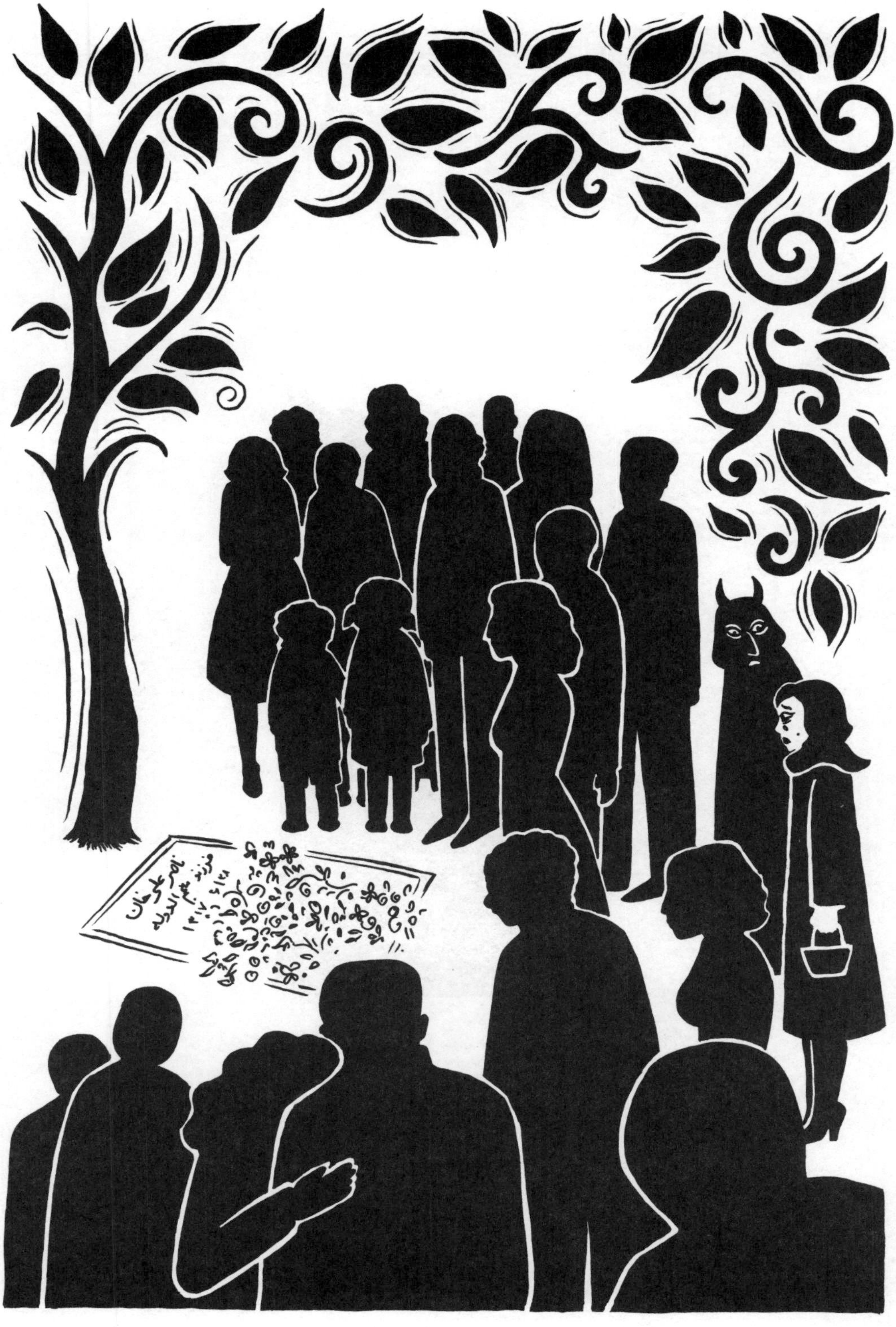

ABOUT THE AUTHOR

Marjane Satrapi was born in 1969 in Rasht, Iran. She now lives in Paris, where she is a regular contributor to magazines and newspapers throughout the world, including *The New Yorker* and *The New York Times*. She is the author of several children's books, *Embroideries*, and her critically acclaimed and internationally best-selling memoir published in two volumes as *Persepolis: The Story of a Childhood* and *Persepolis 2: The Story of a Return*. *Persepolis* has been translated into more then twenty languages, was a *New York Times* Notable Book, and received the Harvey Award for best American edition of foreign material and an Alex Award from the American Library Association. *Persepolis* is also being made into an animated feature film, cowritten and codirected by Ms. Satrapi, to be distributed by Sony Picture Classics in 2007.